THE OLD RELIGION
IN THE BRAVE NEW WORLD

The Jefferson Memorial Lectures

Sidney E. Mead

The Old Religion
in the Brave New World

*Reflections on the Relation Between
Christendom and the Republic*

University of California Press
Berkeley · Los Angeles · London

University of California Press
Berkeley and Los Angeles, California
University of California Press, Ltd.
London, England
Copyright © 1977 by
The Regents of the University of California
ISBN 0-520-03322-1
Library of Congress Catalog Card Number: 76-24588
Printed in the United States of America

To the people who are the University of Iowa
because they made the last ten years
of my professional career the most
enjoyable, the most productive,
the most profitable.

". . . how could you be so noble!"
—*Becky to Tom Sawyer*

When the scene is past we think we know it, though there is so much to see, and so little time to see it, that our conceit of knowledge as regards the past is for the most part poorly founded; neither do we care about it greatly, save insofar as it may affect the future, wherein our interest mainly lies.
SAMUEL BUTLER, *Erewhon, or Over the Range*

I who am king of the matter I treat, and who owes an accounting for it to no one, do not for all that believe myself in all I write. I often hazard sallies of my mind which I mistrust, and certain verbal subtleties at which I shake my ears. . . .
MICHEL DE MONTAIGNE, ''Of Vanity''

. . . someone might say of me that I have here only made a bunch of other people's flowers, having furnished nothing of my own but the thread to tie them.
MICHEL DE MONTAIGNE, ''Of Physiognomy''

Contents

Preface

Each lecture in a series delivered over a period of time to a kaleidoscopic succession of audiences, must be designed to stand alone, to make sense apart from its mates. The consequent style has been retained in the five essays in this collection. Each is a separate bead, but all are strung on the same central theme. It is my hope that the effect of the series is cumulative. This is an explanation and apology for the repetition of ideas and materials that occur.

These essays owe their appearance to a host of persons and institutions who risked inviting me to conferences, lectureships, dialogues, and conversations. My thanks are due first to the Jefferson Lecture Committee who honored me with the invitation to give the lectures in 1974. Among the many persons who contributed to their delivery and made our stay on the Berkeley campus a delightful and profitable experience the following are typical. Dean Sanford S. Elberg proved to be an unbureaucratic and congenial official representative of the University. Mrs. Ella Sponseller, acting "for the Dean of the Graduate Division," exhibited before, during, and after our visit an unusual genius in taking care of the numerous details that make such a venture possible.

Professor and Mrs. Henry F. May added a gracious personal touch to our experience of the Berkeley area and campus which we shall long remember. I am particularly indebted to Professor May and to William J. McClung of the University of California Press, Berkeley, whose detailed and thoughtful criticisms of the original manuscript contributed greatly to what is good in its final form.

My first extensive attempt to develop my views of the complex relations between American Christianity and the Republic in which it has been shaped was made in preparation for the Rauschenbusch Lectures given at the Colgate Rochester Divinity School in 1969 under the general title "Religion and America's Continuing Revolution." I recognize my indebtedness to Professor Winthrop S. Hudson and his colleagues who extended the invitation and so set my mind on that track.

My interpretation of Lyman Beecher sprouted while writing my Ph.D. dissertation on his alter-ego, Nathaniel William Taylor, in the late 1930s, and flowered in the 1967 Beecher Lectures I delivered at the Yale University Divinity School on "Lyman Beecher and the Government of God. . . ." Let Professor Sydney E. Ahlstrom, who was our genial host and my incisive critic during our stay at Yale, stand as representative of all his colleagues who proved to be agreeable and helpful companions.

The people of Ball State University, Muncie, Indiana, who invited me to give five public lectures during my stay as the John R. Emens Visiting Professor in the fall of 1975, provided me with a much appreciated opportunity and tangible inducement to lick the manuscript into final form through revision, enlargement, and polishing.

The third chapter of this book, in somewhat different form, was given as one of the three Armstrong Lectures at

Kalamazoo College, Michigan, in October, 1975, and has been published, with the permission of the University of California Press, along with the lectures of Professors Robert N. Bellah and Jerald C. Brauer, in a volume entitled *Religion and the American Revolution,* with Prof. Brauer as editor (Fortress Press, 1976). I profited greatly from the critical comments made by my two fellow lecturers, and by others who attended the conference at Kalamazoo College.

Having mentioned the above, a tender regard for what shreds of originality I can claim leads me to absolve them from all responsibility for my "facts," themes, style of presentation, and writing.

However, lacking the fortitude to stand wholly alone, I do not thus completely absolve Mary Lou Doyle, Editorial Assistant at the School of Religion, University of Iowa, from all such responsibility. For this incarnation of my musings in print has so depended on her editorial skills, gentle excellence in criticism, and remarkable persistence tempered with patience in getting the job done, that simple justice would make appropriate the application of "our" rather than "my" to the finished product.

Finally, let it be said that

> In a subject so copious as this, I am far from supposing it probable that I have made no mistakes, notwithstanding I have used all the care and precaution that I could. If any such be pointed out to me, whether it be by a friend or an enemy, I shall be glad to avail myself of the intimation, in case there should be a demand for a second edition. As some of my materials bear an equal relation to several of the subjects into which the work is divided, the reader will find a repetition of some things, but they are so few, and so useful in their respective places, that it hardly requires an apology. As

to the repetition . . . the importance of the subject must apologize for it. (Joseph Priestley, *An History of the Corruptions of Christianity,* 2 vols. [2nd ed., London: J. Thompson for J. Johnson, 1793], I, xxv-xxvi).

London: J. Thompson for J. Johnson, 1793], I, xxv-xxvi).

> The last thing one settles in
> writing a book is what one should
> put in first.
>
> PASCAL, *Pensées*, #19

Introduction

In any civilization it is man's religious institutions that refresh in him from time to time the will (for it is a matter of will, though not a matter of choice) to retain the presuppositions by whose aid he reduces such experience as he enjoys to such science as he can compass; and it is by dint of these same religious institutions that he transmits these same presuppositions to his children. For if science is "experience" interpreted in the light of our general convictions as to the nature of the world, religion is what expresses these convictions in themselves and for their own sake and hands them on from generation to generation. And it does this . . . whether [or not] we know by means of metaphysical analysis what these convictions are.[1]

Curiosity is the mother Clio. Every historical study is an attempt to provide a satisfactory answer to the question that bugs the author. These essays are addressed to the dual question, why is it that such a large percentage of American citizen-church-members appear to have theologically bifurcated minds, and how did they get that way? An unavoidable subsidiary

1

question is, what is the relation between the two
theologies which they apparently hold in separate
mental compartments?

I have concluded that the two stand in a relation of
mutual antagonism, and are perhaps logically mutually
exclusive. This is to say that practically every species of
traditional orthodoxy in Christendom is intellectually
at war with the basic premises upon which the constitutional and legal structures of the Republic rest. And
if this *is* the case, then every convincing defense of the
one tends to undermine belief in the other. It follows
that every ardent defense of a sectarian orthodoxy tends
at best to confuse the citizen's understanding of the
basic premises of his country's ideals, at worst to undermine his belief in them, in either case to muddle his
identity.

American sectarians have often in effect offered Mr.
and Ms. John Q. Public a choice between being
faithfully Christian or loyally American, by systematically confusing patriotism with idolatrous worship of
"the state." Patriotism means love for what one's
country ideally stands for, not love simply for the
shenanigans of the current administration's domestic
and foreign policies, if any. As Alexander Hamilton
implied in the first Federalist Paper, philanthropy (love
for mankind) is an integral part of American patriotism
(love for one's country). My country right or wrong is
the ultimate idolatry in politics. Love for what the
country stands for is the only reasonable basis for
criticizing what its political leaders are actually doing.
And, as suggested below, insofar as the American
experiment rests on belief in reason and persuasion,
that is, stands for government by the consent of the

governed, it is more on the Christian beam than Christendom has ever been.

There is an unresolved intellectual tension between the theology professed and promulgated by a majority of the sects, and the theology that legitimates the institutional structures of the American democratic way and style of life. Since loyal citizens who aspire also to be faithful church members in such a commonwealth must hold both perspectives, the result is the split minds of many American citizen-church-members.

This I see as one (and perhaps *the)* root cause not only of the confusion evident in the life of the sects for decades, the anemic condition of their theological enterprise, and the general irrelevance of Establishment religion to both the common life and the power centers of the nation, but also of the wasting sickness evident in the inclusive society itself. In terms of the quotation from R. G. Collingwood that heads this Introduction, the theological difference means that the whole enterprise is in danger of collapse because the religious institutions cannot and have not been doing their destined job.

As for my prognosis, it can be stated in the words of Edward W. Cronin, Jr.:

A basic principle of population biology, the Competitive Exclusion Principle as stated by Hardin, explains that whenever two allied forms have a similar ecology and range, one will invariably gain a selective advantage over the other and displace it. The less successful form either becomes extinct or is forced to migrate.[2]

My opinion is that the "selective advantage" lay with the theology of the Republic, if for no other reason than that all must be citizens but being a church member is a matter of free choice. Of course sectarian species of Christianity have not become extinct. But they have survived at the expense of migrating out of the public realm they dominated for centuries and into the impregnable because ultimately inaccessible recesses of individual hearts—the last sure refuge of obscurantism (Chapter II). This internalization or privatization of religion is one of the most momentous changes that has ever taken place in Christendom.

Judged by the most common response to the lectures when given, it seems to be the suggestion that traditional forms of orthodoxy are incompatible with the principles underlying the structures of the Republic that attracts most attention. This I did not anticipate. For I began with the perhaps naive supposition that the mutually exclusive character of the two positions had been obvious at least since Timothy Dwight and those of his ilk launched the attack on "infidelity" around 1800 that inundated "Enlightenment" in the waves of revivalism commonly known as the Second Great Awakening.

But naive or not, two things still seem to me to be so extensively documented as to appear obvious to a majority of those in a position to know: that "infidelity" was driven underground in the United States by around 1830, and that what was and is commonly understood by "infidelity" when used by orthodox sectarians is the theology that legitimates the legal defense of religious pluralism in a commonwealth by a religiously *desectarianized* (not to be confused with "secularized") and neutral civil authority.

Such are the main themes of these essays. To be understood, or at least to be persuasive, they must be seen in the context of a broadly inclusive interpretation of the significant results of the experience of the old Christianity in the brave new world. The general interpretative motif is that of response to new experiences thrust upon the actors by confrontation with a new environment (Chapter I). This, at least since the time of Crèvecoeur, has been the most favored explanation of this strange new man, the American.

In adopting this approach I join the goodly company of those who have seen that the commonly used categories within which the vicissitudes of Christianity in Europe down to the seventeenth century are interpreted with fair adequacy, are neither applicable to, nor adequate for historical understanding and elucidation of religious developments in the United States where, for example, there is neither a "church" nor a "state" in the traditional sense. In this respect the United States is a post-Christendom nation. Therefore, in order to develop my particular themes in a manner as convincing as possible, it has been necessary to wander boldly, albeit often with apprehension, into the preserves of other disciplines and through wide areas of methods and interpretations largely foreign to me.

Further, the habits of a teacher are not eradicable, even if it were desirable to do so. In trying to communicate any idea or point, the good teacher realizes the inadequacy of just stating it, however clear it may seem to him, and the necessity to try to pick up the hearers or readers where they are, and lead them gently down the paths that took the teacher to that particular conclusion. This suggests another reason why the presentation is discursive. I know that pitfalls for the scholar lurk along that route. For unless the teacher really believes something he has nothing to communicate. And as wise but gently cynical old Michel de Montaigne noted long ago in his essay ''Of Cripples,''

> . . . whoever believes anything esteems that it is a work of charity to persuade another of it, and in order to do so does not fear to add out of his own invention as much as he sees to be necessary in his story to take care of the resistance and the defect he thinks there is in the other person's comprehension.[3]

As I worked on these essays I was constantly haunted by the truth of A. N. Whitehead's insight, that ''the prominent facts are the superficial facts,''[4] the froth on the surface of history. But it is also true that only after the prominent facts of one's immediate subject have been ordered out of the primordial chaos (Chapter I, pp. 13-15) can one suggest to his audience the nature of the gulf stream of history on which they float. Because this Introduction is the last thing to be written it is the place for that suggestion.

Whitehead argued that ''one of the greatest intellectual discoveries in the history of religion'' was ''Plato's . . . final conviction . . . that the divine element in the world is to be conceived as a persuasive agency and not as a coercive agency.''[5] This is the ideal ''general form of [all] the forms of thought''[6] about the nature of God, and of man, and of the relation between them, that have appeared in the history of Christianity.

This metaphysical intuition, the ''essence of Christianity,'' is for Christians exemplified in ''the life of Christ as a revelation of the nature of God and of his agency in the world''[7]—that is of reality [''. . . he that hath seen me hath seen the Father'' (John 14:9)].

The problem confronted by the early theologians was that "of the role of the persuasive agency of God" in the world. Plato left a gap between "the World" and "God and his ideas." Christians "decided for the direct immanence of God in the one person of Christ," the doctrine of the second person of the Trinity—and "they also decided for some sort of direct immanence of God in the World generally . . . their doctrine of the third person."[8] Saint Paul clothed these high generalities in the specialized notion that ". . . all things are of God, who hath reconciled us to himself by Jesus Christ," making the essential Christian message "that God was in Christ, reconciling [persuading] the world unto himself . . . and hath committed unto us the work of reconciliation" (II Cor. 5:18-19).

Supposing that the divine agency in the world, the essence of Christianity, is persuasion and not coercion, means that the driving force of Christianity in history, its mission, is to incarnate this ideal in the actuality of all human relations, in all social structures. Christians were to conquer the world without literally slugging it out with the armies of the world. This tempting possibility was rejected in the myth of the third temptation of Jesus (Matt. 4:8-11).

This, then, the great idea and master ideal of Christianity, is rightly invoked as a standard in judging the fidelity of Christians to their destiny.

Whitehead noted that all great ideas "enter into reality with evil associates and with disgusting alliances."[9] When in the fourth century Christians entered such a disgusting alliance with Constantine, "Christendom" was born. And one who judged its defenders by their record thereafter might rightly decide that they confronted those who disagreed with them, not with their professed Master's advice to "Love your enemies," but with the crude and earthy battle cry, "Kill the bastards!" This historical development is the gulf stream of these essays.

In this context it appears that during the eighteenth century in America, those who led the movement to incarnate in civil institutions the ideal of persuasion (government by the consent of the governed; Tocqueville's dogma of the sovereignty of the people), were in their day more representative of Christianity than were the orthodox defenders of Christendom's Established churches, and those who tried to make Christendom's species of institutionalized religiosity part of the Common Law of the land. This, I think, is probably what John Courtney Murray had in mind when he suggested that Protestants and deists used the true Catholic answer in defining the nature of man and in confronting the problem of pluralism and religious freedom (Chapter I, p. 22).

In nineteenth-century dress the confrontation is seen in the profound difference between Lyman Beecher's theological model resting on God's creation of free agents, and Horace Bushnell's model of Christendom's universe wherein *his* Christ was drowning the atheistic nostrums of Jefferson in the "blood, blood, rivers of blood" being spilled in the Civil War (Chapters IV and V).

Having called attention to this long-standing and useful distinction between Christianity and Christendom, I want to emphasize that Christendom's often fossilized religious institutions—what Harvey Cox calls the "signal-heavy bureaucracies, cut off from the freshening sources without which both religion and culture die"[10]—bad as they are, must be given due credit for being the vehicles in which knowledge of the master ideal of Christianity has been kept alive and carried down through the centuries to such "modern" critics as Voltaire, Thomas Paine, Thomas Jefferson, H. L. Mencken, Mr. Cox, and myself. In my terminology all, whether consciously or not, have invoked the true Christian ideal in judging the churches of Christendom.

So I raise a gentle demurrer against Cox's implication that his "signal-heavy bureaucracies" are "cut off from the freshening sources . . ." completely. They are not and cannot be so long as they nourish some spark of esteem for the Bible, the heart of Western culture, the real source of practically all the revolts against the structures of Christendom. Recent attempts by doctors of theology to transplant a new heart into Christendom have not been noticeably more successful than the attempts of doctors of medicine to transplant new hearts into human beings. Emerson, I think, was essentially right: ". . . all attempts to project and establish a Cultus with new rites and forms, seem to me vain. . . . Rather let the breath of new life be breathed by you through the forms already existing. For if once you are alive, you shall find they shall become plastic and new." And his summary remedy has a contemporary ring: "The remedy to their deformity is first, soul, and second, soul, and evermore, soul."[11] The seeds of renewal for the existing churches lie within those churches. Whitehead's conclusion is the right one—although the potent motivational ideas are always found with disgusting allies and evil associates, their "greatness remains, nerving the race in its slow ascent."[12]

Because my use of the words *sect, sectarian,* and *sectarianism* plays an important part in my presentation, some explanation of what I usually mean by them is appropriate.[13] *Sectarianism* is the claim of a group exclusively to be *the* church of Christ on earth and the only ark of salvation. A *sectarian* is one who makes this claim for his species, or sub-species, of Christianity. He exemplifies Christendom's two-category perspective (all "Christian" is good, all "not-Christian" of my species is bad), and confuses his sub-species of religion with religion. The word *sect* I use as apparently eighteenth-century writers commonly did, that is, in a descriptive and not in a pejorative sense. I think the typology of *church* and *sect,* although favored by some very learned sectarians overly impressed by the omniscience of Ernst Troeltsch, has no application to the American situation, and probably reflects nostalgia for the good old snobbish days when orthodox churchmen did not have to tolerate those who differed from them.

. . . one cannot observe strictly all the
usual formalities in making a beginning
under such circumstances.

JONAS MICHAËLIUS, 1628

Americans have rewritten the old epics
and have added myths of their own. From
the Greeks, we've taken the plural gods,
the rape of beauty, the long war, the
wandering and the return. From the
Hebrew and Christian myth, we've taken
the lost garden and the divine man. But
to all this we've added our own national
experience.

ROSS LOCKRIDGE, *Raintree County,* 1948

I

The Old Religion in the Brave New World: New Environment, New Forms

Every particular history must of necessity begin in the
middle, or, more precisely, in the midst, of the vast,
inclusive story of life on this planet. Each is an arbitrary
slice of the great pie. Emerson described the dawn of
self-consciousness, saying, we awake to find ourselves

> In a series of which we do not know the extremes,
> and believe that it has none. We wake and find

ourselves on a stair; there are stairs below us, which we seem to have ascended; there are stairs above us, many a one, which go upward and out of sight. But the Genius which according to the old belief stands at the door by which we enter, and gives us the lethe to drink, that we may tell no tales, mixed the cup too strongly, and we cannot shake off the lethargy now at noonday. Sleep lingers all our lifetime about our eyes, as night hovers all day in the boughs of the fir-tree.[1]

Alfred North Whitehead rehearses the same sentiment in noting that "We do not initiate thought by an effort of self-consciousness. We find ourselves thinking, just as we find ourselves breathing and enjoying the sunset."[2]

Thinking is a self-consciously directed break into the perpetual reverie that characterizes the individual's mind. Disciplined history is a way of thinking about the "footprints on the sands of time" that creates an ordered and useable past. Assuming, as modern historians do under the category of developmentalism, the unbroken continuity of events, any history is a ruthless slashing into the vast tapestry arbitrarily to cut out what to the historian seems a manageable and useful piece of the whole. As Thornton Wilder puts it,

But there is only one history. It began with the creation of man and will come to an end when the last human consciousness is extinguished. All other beginnings and endings are arbitrary conventions— makeshifts parading as self-sufficient entireties, diffusing petty comfort or petty despair. The cumbrous shears of the historian cut out a few figures and a brief passage of time from that enormous tapestry. Above and below the laceration, to the right and left

of it, the severed threads protest against the injustice, against the imposture.[3]

Thinking is mankind's instrument for creating an
order, a universe, out of and in the midst of the
surrounding chaos, the aboriginal darkness in which
our origins are buried and out of which, according to
that old Scotch prayer, "ghoulies and ghosties / and
long-leggety beasties / and things that go bump in the
night" continually assail our peace of mind.

If we are to understand our predicament and destiny
it is important to realize that a sense of "order" is not
a given of the senses, not a result of observation, but a
very fragile creation of the human spirit.[4] In our
tradition the archetypal motivational myth is that of
God's spirit hovering over the dark and formless void,
coaxing out of it, first, the ordered universe and then,
in the image of the gods, man, destined to have
dominion as co-worker with God in the eternal act of
creation—the only secure defense against a catastroph-
ical lapse into the primordial chaos.

A subliminal sense of the possibility of such lapse
makes ours an age of anxiety. Surely each one of us,
however snugly ensconced in the seemingly solid security of our middle-class jobs, cars, houses, insurance
policies, and power lawn mowers, must sometimes in
terror have exclaimed with Macbeth: "To be thus is
nothing, but to be safely thus—."[5] And we love the
comic bumbling of W. C. Fields because his unnerving
experience with unaccountably flexible pool cues, and
the wavering contents of his neatly stacked closets
which threaten to topple over and bury him under
their inherent disarray, make his a kindred soul. "Only
the feet on the rug are firm," says Walter Kerr,

and someone is pulling at the rug. Any man on his way to the office in the morning is a man wondering what is going to go wrong today. Any man on his way home in the evening is a man wondering what has gone wrong today. Home is another of his problems in order.[6]

Christians, in keeping with their archetypal motivational myth, have always felt and often vividly pictured the extreme fragility of their self-created orders both heavenly and of this world. As one striking example we may take Edmund Spenser's "Mutability Cantos" of 1609, wherein the Titaness, Mutability (Change), already having gained recognized dominion over this world of sense experience and empirical evidence, seeks sovereign control over the gods themselves, at which all on earth quake "Fearing lest Chaos broken had his chain / And brought again on them eternal night—."[7]

The issue, of course, is that nature of ultimate reality. The supreme judge, the goddess of Nature, after hearing Mutability's persuasive arguments, points out that while all things hate steadfastness and are ever changing, yet in doing so each forever produces after its own kind, and thus they "work their own perfection" which is constant. And this means, says Dame Nature, that ". . . over them Change doth not rule and reign / But they reign over Change, and do their states maintain."

But this conclusion, so beyond what is observed, rests upon the belief "Of that same time when no more change shall be, / But steadfast rest of all things, firmly stayed / Upon the pillars of eternity."[8] In other words, that order *is* the nature of ultimate reality is a matter of faith, which, as the book of Hebrews has it, alone can "prove the existence of the realities that at present remain unseen."[9] The universal assertion of Christians in all their creeds of belief "in God the Father almighty, *Maker* of heaven and earth" is the affirmation in faith that we live in an ordered universe that is being perpetually generated out of the mysterious void that envelops it.

Only as we perceive this Christian sense of the extreme vulnerability of all tangible order can we understand the frenzied and violent reaction of sectarian Christians to every real or imagined threat to their orthodox theologies and/or the social, political, and economic structures legitimated by them.[10] Always the equanimity of wise old Mother Church has been shattered by such threat, and of her one might say what Hamlet's mother said of the player-Queene, "The lady doth protest too much, methinks"[11]—and say it for the same reason.

This, I suggest, is necessary background for an understanding of the plight of Christianity and the Church in the modern world.

The meaning of the modern world for the religious tradition of Christendom was caught with poignant clarity by Walter Lippmann in *A Preface to Morals,* published in 1929. Through Lippmann's complex orchestration of the corroding effects of "The Acids of Modernity" on traditional Christian beliefs and their consequent social structures, runs the constant theme, "Whirl is King." Without stretching imaginative apprehension to the breaking point, we may think of *A Preface to Morals* as a classic sequel to Edmund Spenser's "Mutability Cantos" in which Dame Nature on second thought acknowledges Mutability's claim of right to rule over the gods themselves; which is to say that it is recognized that the nature of ultimate reality *is* mutability, that the axis of what Loren Eiseley calls mankind's "invisible environment" is no longer fixed,[12] that the metaphysical intuition of eternal substances must yield to that of "Process."[13]

On the surface this vast oceanic shift was made manifest in evolutionism. And many a clergyman and scholar has surfboarded over the attendant controversies, intellectually unaware of the cultural depths beneath them, albeit correctly feeling that thoroughgoing developmentalism effectively dethrones both the orthodox Christian's and the deist's Deity who "made the world and governs it by his providence."[14]

The United States emerged in an era when, as has often enough been said, an old world was not yet dead and a new was struggling to be born: the "age of revolutions" which, with John Adams, we may date as 1775 to 1815.[15] Seymour Martin Lipset has rightly dubbed ours "the first new nation."[16] It was a new kind of commonwealth in Christendom religiously, primarily because the founders had realized that if there was to be a *United* States made up of the heterogenous thirteen colonies, it could have no nationally Established church such as fourteen centuries of Christendom's teaching had held was essential.

In the environment provided by such a strange new commonwealth Christians, if they were to survive as such at all, had to adapt[17] their institutions and their institutionalized (and sometimes fossilized) ways of thinking to meet the exigencies of a world they did not make and only grudgingly permitted to be born. The history of the old religion in the brave new world is the complex story of the nature and results of such adaptations. Naturally as the old Christianity was poured into the new environmental molds it assumed new shapes.

History as a disciplined way of thinking about the past, is one of the many efforts to erect bastions of meaning in our perennial war against chaos, hopefully to overcome it and create a secure island of meaning and discourse in the midst of surrounding meaninglessness—to forestall ''the experience of nothingness'' which threatens to overwhelm us.[18]

More concretely, if we ask why study history—what is its purpose—we can hardly do better in reply than to quote Abraham Lincoln's observation in the famous ''House Divided Speech'': ''If we could first know where we are, and whither we are tending, we could better judge what to do, and how to do it.''[19] Insofar as this *is* the purpose, every history is useful only as it gives us such a useable past.

Recognized ignorance is the mother of historical study, for in it curiosity is conceived, and born in the form of questions that demand answers. The archetypal question is, ''where were they, and how did they get there,'' or, if the history is our history, ''where are we, and how did we get here?'' The multi-dimensioned kind of knowledge that is history is made up of the countless more-or-less interrelated answers to that type of question endlessly applied. These answers in the form of theses are made plausible by adherence to accepted rules of evidence in producing them. This implies that our history of any one time and place is the informed opinion of those in a position to know.

It is not entirely fictional to say that back of this series of essays is the curiosity aroused by a study sponsored by the three largest Lutheran synods which allegedly revealed that while 75% of Lutheran church members asserted that belief in Jesus Christ was absolutely essential for salvation, 75% also asserted that all roads lead to God and it does not matter which way one takes. Assuming, as I still do, that the Lutheran denominations are the least theologically eroded of all the Protestant groups in our land, it seemed to me striking that apparently half of their members at least could hold two mutually exclusive theological positions at the same time. This seemed to me an unhealthy situation.

From long study of religious developments in America, my somewhat informed opinion is that these Lutheran church members are fairly typical of a majority of the members of all the other denominations. And, assuming that intellectual coherence and logical consistency are among the accepted tokens of mental and spiritual health, such widespread intellectual bifurcation suggests an endemic mental abnormality in our culture, and prepares one to expect attendant psychogenic oddities in the behavior of the overtly pious. And that really poses a question for the historian. If this *is* the situation, how did we Americans get that way? That is the question I propose to mull over in these essays, and, please note, I do not say that I am able to answer it. But, as we old pro's in Academe happily say, perhaps I can leave you confused on a higher level because you have become aware of the importance of the question.

Those who have read Erik Erikson's books will recognize that this way of putting the question calls for a "case history," which Erickson distinguishes from a "life history" on the basis of their different purposes. A "case history" assumes, or postulates, malfunctioning, and "gives an account of what [apparently] went wrong with a person and why the person fell apart or stopped developing. . . ."[20] Its primary purpose lies in the hope that apprehension of what went wrong may enable and induce the person to set things right again. When we substitute the words "ecclesiastical institution" for the word "person" in Erikson's sentences, the applicability of the approach to the historical study of churches in which at least half the members seem to be theologically schizophrenic becomes obvious.

How did we Americans get that way? The answer depends on noting that when an American asserts that belief in Jesus Christ is essential for salvation, he speaks as one programmed by exposure to Christendom's orthodox tradition of centuries standing. But when he asserts that all roads lead to God and are equally valid, he speaks as the creature of an eighteenth-century "Enlightenment" perspective that legitimated the foundational premises of the Republic. The two perspectives have thus far seemed mutually exclusive, but perhaps this is only because few Christian thinkers have given the issue serious attention. Meantime the differences remain unresolved in the spirit (mind-heart) of those who aspire to be both loyal citizens and faithful church members. Hence their symptoms of bifurcated minds.

But if, as I suppose, this is the case, and if the two perspectives are deemed irreconcilable, then it follows that there is a sense in which all persuasive defenses of sectarian Christianity tend to undermine the citizen's belief in the basic premises on which the Republic rests; *or* undermine his confidence in the necessity for Christian exclusiveness; *or,* what is perhaps most common, erode his belief in all systematically ordered models of "the nature of things." Exploration of the first of these possibilities is the chief, but not the only, thrust of what follows in this and the subsequent essays.

John Adams said there was a sense in which the revolution that eventuated in the War for Independence and the dissolution of the bonds that had bound the thirteen colonies to England actually began when the first permanent settlers set foot on the new land.[21] A first seed was sown by Jonas Michaëlius who in August 1628, shortly after his arrival as the first Dutch Reformed minister in New Netherlands, explained to a friend in Holland who had criticized his departing from the strict order of his church in administering the Lord's Supper, that "One cannot observe strictly all the usual formalities in making a beginning under such circumstances" as existed in the colony.[22]

Seventeen years later Nathaniel Ward (1578–1652), speaking as "The Simple Cobler of Aggawam in America" anxious to "mend his Native Country, lamentably tattered, both in the upper-Leather and sole," flatly stated the then prevailing ideal of a commonwealth in Christendom: "there is no Rule given by God for any State to give an Affirmative toleration to any false Religion, or Opinion whatsoever; they *must connive* in some Cases, but may not concede [in principle] in any."[23]

One hundred and thirty-seven years later (i.e., 1782), J. Hector St. John de Crèvecoeur asked the question that has echoed down through our history: "What then is the American, this new man?" and answered correctly, "He is either an European, or the descendant of an European" who, because of his experience in the New World, "is a new man, who acts upon new principles" and "must therefore entertain new ideas, and form new opinions."[24]

The year Crèvecoeur's *Letters . . .* were published Benjamin Franklin, presuming to give valuable "Information to Those Who would Remove to America," warned that it is a country "where people do not inquire concerning a Stranger, *What is he?* but, *What can he do?* If he has any useful Art, he is welcome; and if he exercises it, and behaves well, he will be respected by all." Then, revealing keen understanding of the religious climate of opinion in the new land, Franklin added: "The People have a saying, that God Almighty is himself a Mechanic, the greatest in the Univers [*sic*]; and he is respected and admired more for the Variety, Ingenuity, and Utility of his Handyworks, than for the Antiquity of his Family."[25]

Almost two centuries later, in 1961, James Baldwin wrote that by living in Paris he discovered that the society in which he had been formed was governed, as are all societies, by "hidden laws" that made it, and him, different from European and African peoples and individuals.[26]

Yet because Americans were and are the descendants of those from other continents and countries, one must conclude with Crèvecoeur that the differences are due to the experience of the old man in the New World situation. Michaëlius is typical of those who immediately recognized that the ecclesiastical forms and social patterns of the Old World could not be strictly adhered to in the New. And as he accommodated his Dutch Reformed practices to the exigencies of the incipient colonial pluralism he adjusted his thinking to explain and defend the changes. As Christian he was on the way to becoming Crèvecoeur's "new man."

All up and down the colonial coast the ideal and expectation of the first planters, English, Dutch, Swedes, was that the ecclesiastical forms developed through centuries of experience in Europe would be perpetuated in the New World. Everywhere charters, laws, and instructions (with the exception of Maryland and, later, Rhode Island) demanded religious uniformity, but nowhere as clearly as by the founders of Massachusetts Bay for whom Nathaniel Ward spoke.

But even Ward recognized the necessity to "connive in some cases," that is, to recognize that sometimes a deviant form is so trivial that it represents no threat, or so virulent and powerful that to suppress it, as principle demanded, would so disrupt the social and political structure as to endanger the existence of the commonwealth itself. Ward recognized what had long been recognized, that it would be "Madness to saue a part, and lose the whole."[27] What does it profit if although the operation be a success the patient dies? But connivance, whether because the deviant is judged too trivial to be dangerous or too virulent to be safely attacked, meant that what was deemed wrong in principle was given the tacit approval that would flower in religious freedom.

Religious pluralism[28] came to prevail as, in effect, between the planting of the first permanent English colony in 1607 and acceptance of the Constitution and

First Amendment in 1787–1789, "connivance" was somehow elevated into that positive principle of religious freedom that has guided the Supreme Court's successive definitions of the meaning when applied to specific issues of the principles embodied in Article Six and the Amendment. Mr. Justice Frankfurter stated it clearly in his opinion in the Gobitis Case of 1940, calling it the principle of the "plurality of principles which, as a matter of history, underlies protection of religious toleration."[29]

Of course the concept of a plurality of principles which implies that all theologies are equally valid, and perhaps equally true,[30] is overtly anathema to the sectarians of Christendom, and covertly so even to polite and sophisticated absolutists who reveal their true position by railing against "Christianity in general."

The experience of the colonial European-embryo-American made connivance in religious deviation a necessary condition of survival in every colony, and survival even in a land rich in natural resources demanded skilled workmen. Captain John Smith, fighting for the life of the Virginia colony, begged its supporters in England to send skilled workers,[31] thus anticipating what Franklin was to note almost two centuries later, that the important thing in the New World was not what a person was, but what he could and would do.

I suppose it likely that when I was a graduate student in the Divinity School of the University of Chicago four decades ago the dictum that theology is "transcendentalized politics" penetrated my subconscious mind and programmed me to suppose that one's

conception of "God" reflects what he considers primarily important for the life of mankind. And perhaps
that is why I find congenial Franklin's insight that his
Americans tended to admire God "more for the
Variety, Ingenuity, and Utility of his Handyworks,
than for the Antiquity of his Family." And I think it
significant that the first message an American thought
of to be sent across the ocean by telegraph was, "What
hath God wrought?"

It is written that the gods made man in their image
and after their likeness, and invited him to be co-
worker with them in the creation of his own destiny.
The obverse of this is that societies create their concepts
of the attributes and character of the god they worship
in the likeness of the pressing practical problems of
their time and place. As in early America the consum-
ing interest in persons was in what they could do, it
was natural that early New England Puritan historians
from Edward Johnson (1598–1672) through Cotton
Mather (1663–1728) tended with an assist from the Old
Testament, to trim the multi-dimensioned God of, for
example, William Langland's *Piers the Ploughman*
(*c.* 1370) into a "wonder-working" deity engaged
primarily in whipping out "remarkable providences"
as easily for the edification and consolation of His saints
as for the punishment of the wicked on Michael
Wigglesworth's ever present as well as future *Day of
Doom . . . !*

It was of course a matter of emphasis, as are all the
many different versions of Christianity made manifest
in the thousands of conflicting theologies and institutions that have fought viciously for supremacy in the
name of the meek and lowly suffering servant of them

all. For the boundaries of permissible Christian doctrine remained pretty much as defined at the Council of Nicaea in 325. One may agree with the author of the article in the *Encyclopedia Britannica* that the voting that determined what was to be orthodox does not reflect ''the inward convictions'' of the members, but rather was due ''partly to indifference, partly to the pressure of the imperial will'' of Constantine.[32] For the Emperor, who recognized the salutary influence a unified Christian church might exert in the Empire, demonstrated to winners and losers alike the efficacy of impressively vestmented coercive power in the settling, if not the solving, of divisive theological issues. It was a lesson that actual and would-be orthodox leaders would never forget. And as the pagan guts of the Roman Empire decayed, Christians moved into the shell (as the bees moved into the carcass of the lion Samson had slain), donned the imperial robes, and became Princes of the Church who demanded the pinch of incense on *their* altar as ardently as and more ruthlessly than had the pagan, Diocletian (254–313). Such leaders of Christendom, like the Gospel's ''poor,'' seem destined to be ever with us.

The unbroken historical continuity from the Emperor Constantine in 325 to those for whom Nathaniel Ward spoke in 1647 can be traced in the line of Christendom's leaders who dressed Christ in Caesar's armor, and scrambled sacred with profane, ecclesiastical with civil, the sword of steel with the sword of the Spirit, and the state with the Church. During all those centuries, throughout the West, Christians practically without exception assumed that the being and continued well-being of a commonwealth depended upon overt uniformity of religious belief and practice, thus making the forceful suppression of heresy and all schismatic religious dissent the first law of survival for a commonwealth. They assumed that the set of principles that motivated the general participation must be "Christian" in their sectarian sense.

This meant, in modern terminology, that from the fourth to the eighteenth century "specialized religious institutions" had a legal "monopoly [in] defining the sacred cosmos" that legitimated the social, political and economic orders of the society.[33] Such monopoly was natural in the context of the medieval view of the hierarchical arrangement of the cosmos, in which "the whole chain of being is realized in scales of being and value" and "the first cause operates through secondary causes; 'The king and Lord of the heavens,' says Thomas, 'ordained from eternity this law: that the gifts of his providence should reach the lowest things by way of those that lie between.' "[34]

The family quarrel in the household of Christendom that we call the Reformation broke the religious and moral monopoly of the universal and transnational Catholic church, and the revolutions that followed in the seventeenth and eighteenth centuries broke the religious monopolies of the Established churches in the new nations.

Rejecting the balanced triune authority of Catholic Christianity, Scripture, tradition, and Church (reflecting "the Catholic doctrine that a living Church is required to interpret lifeless documents"[35]), Protestants defined their fundamental premises in the slogans, no authority but the Scriptures and the right of private judgment in their interpretation. This was to undermine in principle the one heretofore accepted institutionalized standard that had guided the cultural and social life of Christendom. For no such code can be maintained without an institution in the society generally recognized as having the final authority to interpret what it means when applied to specific issues that arise and require adjudication between individuals exercising their private judgment in its interpretation.[36]

Protestant churches managed to exist only insofar as Protestants failed in their institutions to act upon what they seemed to profess to believe—that individuals had the right to private judgment in interpreting what the Bible meant and required. The many Protestant historical creeds, confessions, and excommunications bear eloquent witness to this—as does the present World Council's requirement of profession of belief in Jesus Christ as God and Savior for fellowship and co-operation.

Certainly no right of private judgment was officially recognized in the passionately Protestant England of Elizabeth I (1558–1603) and James I (1603–1625) when God and monarch were so merged that early laws for Virginia were "declared against what Crimes soeuer, whether against the diuine Majesty of God, or our soueraigne, and Liege Lord, King James."[37]

But one may guess that as ministers and magistrates in the first Dutch and English plantings discovered with Michaëlius that one could not rigidly adhere to the old forms "under such circumstances," that the latent principle of private judgment was increasingly applied to isolated religious societies more than to individuals, and bolstered the necessity to connive in deviance as it "sicklied o'er" the resolution to maintain uniformity. Certainly efforts to do so seem often to have been half-hearted, as we might expect from the residents of a house so divided against itself.

Meantime during the seventeenth and eighteenth centuries the main currents of thought among the intellectuals converged on the theological legitimation of private judgment as an unalienable right, but at the expense of discarding the keystone of the orthodox Christian arch—the Bible as the one and only revelation of God for the guidance of mankind to "salvation" through Jesus Christ, truly God, truly human, and only Savior.

Protestants of course, while insisting upon the right of private judgment, continued to assume the absolute authority of Scripture. As Horace Bushnell described their position, they were rational under the Scriptures. But the new breed of intellectuals presumed to be rational beside, beyond, or without the Scriptures, and in doing so they created a new religion. Crane Brinton describes the emergence of this form:

> The basic structure of Christian belief survived, however, not without heresies and schisms, until, roughly, the late seventeenth century when there arose in our society what seems to me clearly to be a new religion, certainly related to, descended from, and by many reconciled with, Christianity. I call this religion simply Enlightenment with a capital E.[38]

This religion was "new" only in the sense that any intellectual model is new, namely, it was a new configuration of old ideas which may aptly be described

theologically as a truncated form of Christian orthodoxy—a radical monotheism, or a Unitarianism of the
First Person and without Biblical authority. Its pro-
ponents might have said with Blaise Pascal, "Let no
one say that I have said nothing new; the arrangement
of the subject is new. When we play tennis, we both
play with the same ball, but one of us places it
better."[39] Vis-à-vis the emerging modern world, the
representatives of "Enlightenment" religion were plac-
ing the ball more effectively.

What is most significant historically is that for the
first time in Christendom the people of a commonwealth were offered an authentically religious alternative to orthodox Christianity, and their right to accept
and propagate it defended by the civil authority.[40]

Here we touch the heart of the revolutions that
manifest the birth pangs of the "modern" world,
when leaders asserted that where commonwealths were
concerned the dogmas of Christendom's past were
contrary to the needs of the revolutionary present and
future and people must think and act anew. It was the
theology of "Enlightenment" in Brinton's sense that
legitimated the thrust of the Declaration and the
constitutional structures of "the first new nation" in
Christendom.

As the widespread revolt against the churches of
Christendom took place, most of the Christian theologians turned back to pre-eighteenth century formula-
tions for the explanation and defense of their species of
orthodoxy, and thus made theology itself a shoo-in for
creeping irrelevance in the modern world. Whitehead
referred to this era as the time in history when "the
clergy of the western races began to waver in their

appeal to constructive reason'' as defined in the main
currents of thought in their world.[41]

The consequent polarization of the religious and
intellectual lives of the country becomes increasingly
evident from around the middle of the eighteenth
century. The beginning of the drift apart is suggested
by *The Testimony of the President, Professors, Tutors
and Hebrew Instructor of Harvard College in Cambridge Against the Reverend Mr. George Whitefield,
and his Conduct,* published in 1744.[42] Whitefield's
then innovative manner of revival preaching, which has
since become the classic and accepted style, can hardly
be dignified as an appeal to constructive reason.[43]

The continuation of the drift apart is implicit in the
famous controversy between Charles Chauncy and
Jonathan Edwards over the nature of true religion. It
becomes clearer with the launching of the often-called
''godless'' state universities beginning in the 1790s to
rival the denominationally controlled colleges. The
Dartmouth College decision of 1817, which turned
back the attempt to gain state control of the private
colleges, was a Pyrrhic victory, for it implied the
independence of the private college from denominational as well as state control and helped pave the way
to ever more complete separation of education from its
religious roots.

The Girard Will Case decision in 1844 legally freed
the universities from the control even of what Daniel
Webster called in his plea that ''general, tolerant
Christianity'' which has renounced ''the sword and the
fagot'' (but apparently not the coercive power of the
law). From that point on it was clear that even ''a
purely secular, not to say unreligious'' educational

institution would be sheltered under the wings of the Constitution.[44]

This laid bare the direct clash in principle between the premises that undergirded the legal structure of the Republic and the premises of that species of Christianity which the opponents of the Girard Will Case sought to establish as "basic to the Common Law" of the land. And insofar it helped to nudge the nation's dominant institutionalized religiosity out of the public sphere and consign it to increasing irrelevance in the decision-making centers of the commonwealth.

. . . those gracious influences which the saints are subjects of . . .
are entirely above nature . . . things which no improvement
of those qualifications, or principles that are natural . . . will ever
bring men to; because they not only differ from what is natural
. . . in degree and circumstances, but also in kind.

JONATHAN EDWARDS, 1746

It is a ruinous teaching for any society . . . which persuades
the people that religious belief is enough, by itself and without
morals, to satisfy divine justice. Practice makes us see an
enormous distinction between devoutness and conscience.

MICHEL DE MONTAIGNE, ''Of Physiognomy''

II

The Separation of Salvation from Social Responsibility

In the first essay I suggested that the ''order'' that we
presuppose in all our undertakings is a very fragile
creation of the human spirit—more a matter of faith
than of observation[1]—and that the discipline of history
is the aspect of that creative effort devoted to the
making of a sensibly ordered and therefore understandable and useable past. In our culture the archetypal
motivational myth is that of mankind as co-worker with
God continuously hovering over the primordial chaos,
creating a universe. It is, as Edmund Spenser expressed
it, ''An huge eternal *Chaos,* which supplyes / the
substances of natures fruitfull progenyes.''[2]

My interpretative motif is "experience," which means that, postulating an entity with a definite character that has persisted in time (Christianity) we are to look for an explanation of its peculiarities in a particular time and place (the United States), at the peculiarities in the environment that it confronted there (e.g., "frontier" and "modern democracy"). It is wisdom to suppose with Horace Bushnell that

> When views of religious truth are advanced which either really or apparently differ from such as are commonly accepted, the difference will often be referable to causes that lie back of the arguments by which they are maintained—some peculiarity of temperament, some struggle of personal history, . . . the assumption or settlement of some supposed law or principle of judgment, which affects . . . all subordinate decisions.[3]

It has become a truism in intellectual circles that human beings live always in two environments at the same time—the natural or physical environment which seems "out there," and the "invisible environment" which exists only in their brains. The individual "was not made truly human until, in infancy, the dreams of the group, the social constellation amidst which his own orbit was cast, had been implanted in the waiting, receptive substance of his brain."[4] This means that "No man ever looks at the world with pristine eyes. He sees it edited by a definite set of customs and institutions and ways of thinking. Even in his philosophical probings he cannot go behind these stereotypes; his very concepts of the true and the false will still have reference to his particular traditional customs."[5] From this perspective, now generally accepted, "there is not a fact and an observer, but a joining of the two in an observation. This is the fundamental unit of physics: the actual observation . . . event and observer are not separable."[6]

What I mean by "religion" exists in the "invisible environment"—man's "secret universe of his own creation" peopled with "unseen gods, the powers behind the world of phenomenal appearance."[7] For the understanding of religion in this context, knowledge of what people thought they were doing and why they were doing it is more important than what as a matter of "fact" they did. The historical study of religion yields that kind of knowledge.

One explains what people did, and what people do, by reference to their motives.[8] And human beings are motivated when confronted with challenging aspects of their surroundings by what they *think* the situation to be. And what persons think their situation to be at any time and place is determined by the reality[9] in which they are living; that is, by the contents of the invisible environment in which they live and through which they "see" all experience.

The most obvious characteristic that makes our modern "out there" religious environment different from that which prevailed in Christendom until the eighteenth century is pluralism. On the surface religious pluralism means a multiplicity of different and conflicting religious groups and organizations in the society.[10] But more important is that the forms of each of these sects makes manifest an invisible environment incarnated in its forms, which for the sect's devotees determines the "reality" in which they live.

These sects were transplanted from all the diverse countries and cultures of the Old World, and, as Philip Schaff observed a century and a quarter ago, they are here "fermenting together under [the] new and peculiar conditions"[11] of this strange new commonwealth with religious freedom defended by the civil authority. This means, as anyone who is at all reflective has discovered, that we can never safely assume that another person, however close to us, is actually living in the same world of reality that we inhabit. Surely every married person has a vivid awareness of this.

In formal terms this means that in a pluralistic society all perception is selective, which sociologist Peter L. Berger says "means that in any situation, with its nearly infinite number of things that could be noticed, we notice only those things that are important for our immediate purposes. The rest we ignore."[12] In my words, selective perception is determined by what is in the person's or group's invisible environment. And because these differ one from another, in all our relations with other persons we can never safely assume that they see what we see in the environment, value what we value, like what we like, fear what we fear, or are "rational" in our way.

Thus pluralism forced upon Americans the necessity consciously to work at creating their communities, their universes of discourses if they were to accomplish anything requiring concert of action.[13] As a result of this experience the concept of "freedom" that emerged in America was quite different from that generally prevalent in Europe. In the latter, freedom was defined primarily as reconciliation to the necessity to live within existing social orders, which orders incarnated the applied ramifications of "the great chain of being" concept.[14] In America, on the other hand, the concept of "freedom" has commonly implied escape from real or supposed thralldom to institutions.[15] And this means that the pressures inherent in the American social situation push us more and more into the complete rationalization of all human relations, and the consequent triumph of techniques. The great historian of Roman Catholicism in the United States, Monsignor John Tracy Ellis, recognizing this, wittily noted that when the Roman Catholic church in the United States was inundated with Roman Catholics of many different ethnic, national, cultural, and class backgrounds, "willy-nilly" it became "catholic in the broadest sense."[16]

Of course, as long as there have been humans *as* humans, the necessity to work at creating communities and universes of discourse has been recognized and made tangible in initiation rites and educational systems. The difference in this respect between our modern and preceding societies is one of degree and technique and not of kind. At least since the time of Plato, the live question has been, not this necessity, which was assumed, but the means to be used. Shall it be coercion or persuasion primarily?

The modern world, out of deference to the conception of the nature of human nature that came to prevail in the eighteenth century, has opted for persuasion. This is reflected in the revolutionary slogan that had, and still has, such potent motivational power: government by the consent of the governed, currently perhaps more often stated as the principle of self-determination.

Inasmuch as revolution means that "the people" take the sovereign power into their own hands—and is in that sense an incarnation of what Tocqueville called "the dogma of the sovereignty of the people"[17]—the American system is an attempt to institutionalize perpetual and peaceful revolution.[18] For under it all the sovereign power is periodically and systematically, albeit symbolically, returned into the hands of "the people" in regular elections.

So widely has "consent" been accepted as the operational principle in the modern world that it is the use of force to maintain uniformity of belief and practice that has to be explained, justified, apologized for, if the person, or church, or nation is to retain a decent respect in the opinion of mankind.

Of course recognition of the principle of consent did not necessarily lead to the conclusion that government ought to be democratic—as any reader of Thomas Hobbes' *Leviathan* knows. But for my point, what *is* significant is that Hobbes apparently deemed it wise in 1651 to defend absolute monarchy with the argument that it was so obviously the only effective defense against that state of "warre, as is of every man against every man" that it was the choice of the people expressed in "Pacts and Covenants."[19]

The hometown of principles is in man's invisible environment. When therefore we note that the principle of consent became almost universally recognized, if not always honestly accepted, we are noting one of the huge and fundamental shifts that took place within the invisible environment in which Western man has lived. Karl Jaspers has dubbed the era when that shift took place, the "Axial period" (roughly 800 to 200 B.C.) of human history.[20]

Christianity was conceived during that period when, as Henry Bamford Parkes expounds it,

> thinkers . . . for the first time in human experience, began with man as an individual, asked themselves fundamental questions about the meaning and purpose of his existence, and attempted to answer them in rational terms.[21]

Out of this reflection came the concept of the individual as distinct from the tribe; his individuality rooted in his personal relation to, even identification with, a transcendent universal (commonly called "God") to which he was primarily responsible here and hereafter. As Parkes notes,

> . . . the true expulsion from Eden . . . in the original Hebrew legend was due not merely to man's disobedience but also to the fact that by eating the fruit of the forbidden tree he had come to know good and evil and had thereby acquired a moral independence. . . .[22]

And because such moral independence enabled him to distinguish between good and evil, it forced upon him the necessity to choose whom and what he would serve.[23] He was ushered into the terrible freedom that has plagued him ever since. Here is the mythological statement of the origin of the principle of consent.

This principle, explicit in early Christianity, was expressed in the phrase, "we ought to obey God rather

than man'' (Acts 5:29). To be sure, during the following centuries the ''God'' of Christians has worn many
different masks, assumed many different shapes, been
called by many different names. But throughout the
years that sentiment, often in the guise of higher law
doctrine, has sparked every revolt and revolution.

Asserting this principle, Christians began by defying
the heretofore assumed power of a tribal community to
force individuals to conform to the tribe's beliefs,
rituals, practices. But as Whitehead observed, even
''great ideas enter into reality with evil associates and
with disgusting alliances,'' and often ''centuries, sometimes thousands of years, have to elapse before thought
can capture action.''[24]

When Christians accepted the alliance with Constantine and the Roman Empire, evil because it made
Jesus' kingdom-not-of-this-world the tool of very this-
worldly empires, they reverted to the old principle of
coercion. In doing so they repeated the fatal error so
often condemned by the Jewish prophets of putting
their hope for salvation in alliances with the militarily
powerful. At that point ''Christendom'' was born, and
thereafter, contrary to their true principle, for fourteen
centuries with spectacular pomp and circumstance, they
depended on violence and coercion, purportedly to
build and maintain the kingdom of the one they
worshipped as the Prince of Peace.

It is said that nothing succeeds like success, and the
success of such coercion was impressive. For ''in literature and philosophy [the creatures and creators of
man's invisible environment], Christianity [I would say
''Christendom'' had] won a total victory'' by the end

of the fifth century, and "not for more than a thousand years would it be possible for any citizen of a Christian state to advocate rejection of any of its basic doctrines."[25]

It was that fourteen centuries of Western history, smeared with the blood of those who consciously or inadvertently deviated from the current orthodoxy, that those we call the founders of the Republic confronted, successfully attacked, and launched "the first new nation" in Christendom. It was "new" because where religion was concerned it was launched on what seems to have been the pre-Christendom Christian principle of sole dependence on the sword of the Spirit, the Word of God.

By that time the idea that Christian doctrine and practice must be defended with the sword of steel, and that the being and continued well-being of a commonwealth depended on uniformity of belief and practice within it, had become so much a part of the orthodox bag that it is almost impossible to find a defender of the principle of overt religious freedom for everyone in the churches of Christendom. We take a cue from John Courtney Murray's brilliant insight in saying that in the eighteenth century it was deistically inclined "infidels" (from the orthodox perspective) who enunciated and "used" the true "Catholic answer" to the problem of pluralism in a commonwealth.[26] As Jefferson noted, that answer meant that henceforth the only permissible means of settling theological differences and overt conflicts between the religious sects would be reason and persuasion.[27] In other words, for the first time in Christendom the civil authority was *de-sectarianized* and became in principle neutral vis-à-vis all the particularistic claims of the many sects. Under a government of laws such neutrality was necessary in principle when it devolved upon the civil authority to adjudicate the differences between the religious sects that threatened to disrupt the civil order. The obverse side of this was that sectarian dogmas and beliefs were made irrelevant to one's being and status as a citizen of the Republic. As Jefferson said, our "civil rights" as citizens "have no dependence on our religious opinions, any more than our opinions in physics or geometry. . . ."[28]

Because from the sectarian's perspective religion is an all-or-nothing matter, there can be no neutrality where his species of orthodoxy is concerned. Therefore it is impossible for him to conceive of a religiously neutral civil authority. If it is not overtly "Christian" according to his sectarian definition it perforce must be "infidel," "atheist," "godless," or, as the sophisticated now commonly say, "secular." Jefferson had such sectarians in mind when he complained that "They wish it to be believed that he can have no religion who advocates its freedom."[29]

For this reason every sectarian defense of the religion of Christendom is at least implicitly an attack on a fundamental principle of the Republic which tends to undermine the citizen's belief in it. I suppose, for example, that to say that the Supreme Court is promulgating a "secular religion" implies that the decision has not valid legitimation in Scripture, Christian tradition, or "the nature of things," and is therefore un- or anti-Christian.

And this brings us full circle back to those Lutheran church members noted in Chapter I, with their minds divided and presumably their loyalties torn between what their churches require faithful members to profess, and what the structure of their Republic implies for reflective citizens. It is said on high religious authority that a house divided against itself cannot stand. Edward W. Cronin, Jr., clothed the saying in contemporary scientific dress in noting that

> A basic principle of population biology, the Competitive Exclusion Principle as stated by Hardin, explains that whenever two allied forms have a similar ecology and range, one will invariably gain a selective advantage over the other and displace it. The less successful form either becomes extinct or is forced to migrate.[30]

In American folklore this sentiment was caught in the threat, "this here town just ain't big enough for both of us," which seems aptly to catch the attitude of several absolutist Christians toward the "civil religion."

But I have no desire at this point to pose as a prophet. Rather, as a historian, my interst is in how those Lutherans, and we as a peculiar people, got that way. A complete answer to that question is beyond the possibility of present treatment. I wish to make only a few modest suggestions.

During fourteen centuries of Christendom, contrary to what some always held to be a central principle of the Gospels, the churches freely used coercion to defend their orthodoxies and to hold the wavering faithful in line. During those centuries the theological legitimation of compulsion became part of the invisible environment in which all Christians were nurtured. But at the same time the churches, as continuing institutions in the society, were the vehicles that carried knowledge of the submerged principle of persuasion down through the succeeding generations. So sooner or later it was bound to surface again and alienate more and more individuals from the institutionalized salvation that left such a trail of suffering and blood behind it. This was the time bomb in the very earthly temples of Christendom that exploded during the seventeenth and eighteenth centuries in the widespread revolt against the churches. The gates of hell have never prevailed against the churches of Christendom, but those who threw their own book at them have wrecked elaborate theological structures and leveled institutionalized forms of salvation. This, I think, is nicely illustrated by what happened in those English colonies during the seventeenth and eighteenth centuries. We turn then from the macrocosmic perspective to some of the microcosmic historical details.

If we are to talk about religion and the American Revolution, it is wise to begin with the sharp distinction drawn by John Adams and Thomas Jefferson between the Revolution and the War for Independence. "The war?" asked Adams. "That was no part of the Revolution. It was only an Effect and Consequence of it. The Revolution was in the Minds of the People, and this was effected, from 1760 to 1775, . . . before a drop of blood was drawn at Lexington."[31]

Adams rightly attributed the outbreak and successful outcome of the War for Independence to the fact that a sufficient percentage of the colonial population had come to believe that revolt from the mother country and achievement of independence were necessary and possible, or, in the language of the Rev. Samuel West used in May 1776, that "Providence seems plainly to point to us the expedience, and even the necessity, of our considering ourselves as an independent state."[32] And that meant that a revolution in thinking, that is, in the invisible environment of those people, had taken place.

Second, we should note that "religion" is a very abstract general term that in our society points to no tangible or definite entity.[33] What we are to talk about is the "religious" convictions of these people, and how these beliefs and convictions motivated them to specific actions. People react to what they *think* a situation to be, and what they think a situation to be is a matter of their selective perception determined by what is in their invisible environment.

Third, it is important to keep in mind that the question is the relation of "the old religion," as I have called it, to the "Revolution" in Adams' sense, and that this question is not to be confused (as often it is) with that of the relation of the churches to the War for Independence.

In approaching this question we may best begin, as I noted above, with the situation in which salvation had been institutionalized, formalized, conventionalized. Always for Christians the basic question is that of Saint Paul's jailor, "What must I *do* to be saved?" To say that salvation had been institutionalized means that Paul's answer, "Believe on the Lord Jesus Christ. . . ," had come to mean acceptance of the whole complex bag of theological orthodoxy with its interrelated civil and ecclesiastical forms. In practice this meant that assurance of salvation was premised on observance of certain acts prescribed by one's church. This to be sure is a matter of emphasis. In the tradition assurance ideally is based on the balanced authority of Scripture, Church (that is, the institutionalized community of the faithful), and personal experience of grace. To say that salvation was institutionalized means that the forms of the tangible Church had usurped the authority of Scripture and experience, upsetting the nice balance.

The revolution in religious perspective that is directly related to the political revolution centered on the dogma of the necessity for the use of force to propagate and defend the orthodox institutional forms. But, probably unwittingly, the concerted attack on this particular form in the name of Scripture and personal experience eventuated in undermining unquestioning confidence in all established forms, thus nerving people to question and attack all existing institutions. Hence, as Philip Schaff noted, ''With the universal priesthood comes also a corresponding universal kingship; . . .''[34]

In the English settlements this revolution was carried (not exclusively so of course) in the tidal wave of revivals that swept through all the colonies following *c.* 1725. We have lived so long with the results that it requires some effort to realize the significance of this development in Christendom. Let us begin by looking at the historical development through one of our contemporary interpretations of the present religious scene.

Thomas Luckmann in his book, *The Invisible Religion,* notes as one of our society's most striking phenomena the privatization of religion. He argues that "the new social form of religion . . . is a radically subjective form of 'religiosity.' " The modern sacred cosmos, he continues, "legitimates the retreat of the individual into the 'private sphere' and sanctifies his subjective 'autonomy.' " This separates him from "the primary social institutions" which with their "functional rationality" acquire a seemingly "objective autonomy" and existence apart from him.[35]

This individual is increasingly isolated from his society. Because its institutions are outside his subjective private sphere of reality his sense of participant responsibility tends to evaporate. As I would put it, he becomes a "they" person who passively experiences and suffers the history supposedly created by others, in contrast to those I call "we" persons, those who do have a sense of responsible and meaningful participation in making the history.

"The new social form of religion," unlike forms of the past, Luckmann argues, "does *not* represent the vested interests of a particular social stratum and it is not articulated as a program of political and social action."[36] It merely legitimates the individual's "subjective 'autonomy' "—doing his own thing as it is called. His consciousness is aware only of experiencing a succession of happenings imposed upon him by the system. This is the latest form of solipsism. I agree with Luckmann's thesis respecting the privatization of religion, and presume only to put it into the historical context as I see it.

That family quarrel in the household of Christendom that we call the Reformation or the revolt against the true Church, depending on the species of the genus

Christianity we espouse, selectively opposed the authority of Scripture and experience to that of the
"Church." Hence the slogans on which it was popularly
floated: no authority but the Bible, and the right of
private judgment in its interpretation. Concurrent with
this insistence on the right of private judgment there
emerged the motivational myth of the political revolutions, government by the consent of the governed
institutionalized in the form of covenant. In the
American scenario, which at important points differed
from that of Europe, this meant rational consent to the
practical governmental arrangements deemed necessary
for the common defense of each individual's right to
"life, liberty, and the pursuit of happiness" against
the traditional and always potentially suppressive institutions of society. This represents

> an idea of society as a neutral area within which each
> individual is free to pursue his own development and
> his own advantage as a natural right . . . [and] the
> exertion of social power is thought necessary only in
> so far as it will protect individuals in this basic right
> to set their own course.[37]

These arrangements were legitimated by the "new
religion" (in Crane Brinton's sense) of those we call the
founders (as noted in Chapter I). These statesmen-
political-intellectual leaders were imbued with a vivid
sense of what Alexander Hamilton in the seventy-
eighth Federalist Paper mildly called "the ordinary
depravity of human nature," which at one time led
John Adams to speculate that in the creation of
governments "the best they [mankind] can do is to set
one fool, knave and madman to watch and bind

another fool, knave and madman.''[38] Not unnaturally they mistrusted all institutions as reflectors of human nature with a tendency to become monopolistic and threaten the free individual. The outstanding example before them was the churches.

Most of them would agree with John Adams that while ''Men are rational and conscientious Creatures . . . their passions and Interests generally prevail over their Reason and their consciences: and if Society does not contrive some means of controuling and restrain-[in]g the former the World will go on as it has done.''[39] So, as James Madison had argued in the fifty-first Federalist Paper, the trick was to contrive a government that would not only control the governed but also induce the governors to govern each other. Their solution was to distribute the power in separate but equal branches of the government in such fashion as would appeal to the selfish interests and lust for power of the individuals in each branch jealously to watch the individuals in every other branch lest they abuse the power allotted to them and usurp the power granted the others. This use of ''Ambition . . . to counteract ambition'' Madison wryly described as the ''policy of supplying, by opposite and rival interests, the defect of better motives.''[40] This in Bernard Mandeville's sense was a practical arrangement whereby ''private vices'' were systematically transformed into ''public benefits.''[41]

To reiterate the point, the assumptions on which this structure of government rested were that while social and political institutions were necessary they were always potentially a threat to the individual's natural rights, and that the ''ordinary depravity of human nature'' was the most efficacious principle upon which to rest any government.

In a commonwealth so conceived, the institutions of civil authority, by protecting, thereby encourage what Luckmann called ''the retreat of the individual into the 'private sphere,' '' from which, presumably, only selfish interests and/or ambition for power could lure him. Fawn M. Brodie's Thomas Jefferson is a man oscillating all his long life between these two poles.

Meantime, the revivals beginning in the 1720s in the Jerseys and thereafter spreading through all the colonies, carried a not unrelated revolution in theological perspective and ecclesiastical organization that contributed to the same result. In New England the contrast between the religious perspective of the generation of John Winthrop and John Cotton during the first half of the seventeenth century, and that of Jonathan Edwards and his cohorts a century later, makes the difference starkly clear.

Governor John Winthrop ''On the Attlantic Ocean, On Boarde the Arabella,'' headed for Massachusetts Bay in 1630, explained the venture to those on board with him in an address that has come down to us with the title, ''A Modell of Christian Charity.'' We are, Winthrop argued, ''a Company professing our selues fellow members of Christ'' called ''through a speciall overruleing providence, and a more than an ordinary approbation of the Churches of Christ'' to set up in the wilderness ''a due forme of Government both ciuill and ecclesiastical.'' We have, he continued, ''entered into a Covenant with him [God] for this worke, [and] wee haue taken out a Commission.'' God permitted us ''to drawe our owne Articles [terms],'' and we have

signed the contract by essaying the venture. If we land
safely in Massachusetts that will be God's signature on
the contract; that is, we shall know that we have
correctly interpreted His will in the signs of the times,
and thenceforth we shall be irrevocably bound in this
relation with Deity.[42]

It is important to understand what Winthrop meant
by a "due forme of Government both ciuill and
ecclesiastical." He explained that it was one that would
"bring into familiar and constant practice" that
"which the most in theire Churches maineteine as a
truthe in profession onely." What was that "truthe"?
These people were of the genus Christian and species
Puritan. To them that "truthe" was the absolute
sovereignty of God. They were fleeing from the Anglican species of Christianity because, while its representatives professed belief in the doctrine, they did not
exemplify it in practice, for their church government
was contrary to the form "prescribed in the word,"
which "since the comming of Christ [is] . . . congregational only."[43]

The point here is that from the perspective of their
species of Christianity, the sovereignty of God could be
made manifest on earth only by full incarnation in
social, political, and economic as well as ecclesiastical
institutions. Winthrop was the leader of a total—one
might even say a tribal—community.[44] His theology
clearly legitimated all the institutions necessary for a
complete society, in which, ideally, the laws of the
commonwealth would so closely reflect the command-
ments of God that observance of them would constitute overt, albeit not saving, conformity to His will. As
Robert Baird, the eminent Presbyterian writer, noted in

his *Religion in America,* published in 1843-44, these people "left their native land not so much to promote individual religion as to form Christian societies. . . . Religion with them was not only a concern between man and God, but one in which society at large had a deep interest." There was indeed, he concluded, "a noble patriotism in their religion."[45]

To this species of Puritan the intensely personal experience of conversion which he so greatly emphasized, initiated the convert into social and political responsibility. They believed, as John Cotton explained, that "the church" is fulfilling its true mission only when it "prepareth fitt instruments both to rule, and to choose rulers," that is, persons enabled and made willing by grace to take a responsible part in the government by and for the "saints" that was given form by a covenant.[46] Theirs was the theocratic ideal; belief in "the agency of the saints in expressing God's will for the whole of culture."[47]

If now, we bring down the curtain on that generation and raise it again a century later, zooming in on Jonathan Edwards and his fellow revivalists, we see a radically different religious perspective.

The difference was clearly described by Herbert Wallace Schneider in his book, *The Puritan Mind,* published in 1930.

For Edwards, unlike his New England ancestors, Schneider argued, "religion was essentially a kind of private experience." He "was surprisingly blind to the political philosophy of the Holy Commonwealth" and as for "the Puritan political theory, he nowhere mentions it." While for his New England fathers "religion had been an objective social institution, preoccupied with public concerns; Edwards . . . transformed it into an inner discipline of the emotions." By him the "social and political philosophy" of the early Puritans was given "a private and personal meaning" and wholly "transferred to the inner life of the soul." With Edwards the doctrine of God's absolute sovereignty "had lost its social significance."[48]

Schneider's interpretation is amply supported by Professor Gerhard T. Alexis's probing study of "Edwards' interest in the political community," the conclusion of which is, "very little."[49]

This means that the weight of Edwards' influence was to transfer the wars of the Lord from Cromwell's Nasby fields and Marston Moors to the inner recesses of individual hearts. Proclaiming himself a complete supernaturalist, his theology in principle pushed the doctrine of justification by faith alone to an absolute separation of salvation from one's life in the "natural world." This he made perfectly clear in the treatise on *Religious Affections:*

> . . . it is evident, that those gracious influences which the saints are subjects of, and the effects of God's Spirit which they experience, are entirely above nature, altogether of a different kind from any thing that men find within themselves by nature, or only in the exercise of natural principles; and are things which no improvement of those qualifications, or principles that are natural . . . will ever bring men to; because they not only differ from what is natural, and from every thing that natural men experience, in degree and circumstances, but also in kind; . . . And this is what I mean, by supernatural, when I say that gracious affections are from those influences that are supernatural.[50]

This theology obviously legitimated the privatization of religion, and by completely divorcing salvation from all "qualifications, or principles that are natural," gave the convert the possibility of disengagement with honor from active participation in the political and social life of his society.[51] Conversion, from being initiation into the kind of responsibility for the total community that had characterized the generation of Winthrop and Cotton, became initiation into an exclusive sectarian company of the converted that in principle was at war with the "worldly" social and political affairs of the commonwealth in which it existed. It is for this reason that practically from that time on it was responsible participation in efforts for the community welfare through political action that had to be defended in the prevailing religious circles—as the experience of the "social gospellers" makes abundantly clear.

Admittedly, in some important respects Edwards was not typical of his contemporary revivalists. But in this significant respect he did represent the main thrust of the great awakenings throughout the colonies in all the churches. Everywhere the revivalists in fighting the suppressive civil and ecclesiastical measures invoked against them by defenders of the old orders of Christendom, emphasized the personal, unmediated experience of "the New-Birth" to undermine the people's belief in the saving efficacy inherent in observance of the traditional objective forms of their churches.[52] In doing so of course, they were undermining confidence in all existing institutions and lessening the people's respect for all constituted authority. For at the time, and especially where there were churches established by law, to defy the clergymen was at least symbolically to defy the whole institutional structure of Christendom.

It was in this way that the revivalists contributed to furthering the Revolution "in the Minds of the People" as John Adams defined it. That it was perhaps largely unintentional because they did not realize what they were doing, does not make it any the less significant a part.[53] For as conversion gave individuals the courage to defy constituted authorities, something that is obvious throughout the colonies, they began to act as if all government actually was by sufferance of their consent. Certainly the thrust of the colonial revivals was on the side of the Revolution.

But this must not blind us to the equally important fact that the revivalists' almost exclusive emphasis on personal religious experience as the only basis for "assurance," drove a wedge between the convert's ultimate concern ("salvation") and his concern for the fate of his society. Benjamin Franklin wittily describes his experience of the parting of the ways in his account of the minister who so interested him that "once for five Sundays successively" he attended church to hear the man preach. But, says Franklin, the sermons, being "chiefly either polemic arguments, or explications of the peculiar doctrines of our sect," were "dry, uninteresting, and unedifying, since not a single moral principle was inculcated or enforc'd, their aim seeming to be rather to make us Presbyterians than good citizens."[54] What Franklin was objecting to was the making of institutionalized Presbyterianism an end in itself rather than a means to a larger end—a typical complaint of laypersons against their churches today.

This separation of "salvation" from responsibility for the fate of society under the tutelage of the revivalists helps to explain why political leadership during the eighteenth century gravitated into the hands of those who like Franklin were, from the perspective of orthodox Christians of the time, "infidels," that is, of "Enlightenment" perspective. But, as I have extensively spelled out elsewhere,[55] so long as the pressing, immediate, and practical problem for all the sects was set by the common desire for the religious freedom each group wanted for itself, they followed and supported the political leadership of the "infidels" to its consummation in the Constitution and the First Amendment. But once religious freedom was on the books orthodox leaders recalled what Timothy Dwight so vociferously preached around 1800—that "infidelity" was a vain and deceitful philosophy because it denied that revelation was confined to the Book and that salvation was exclusively by faith in the Lord Jesus Christ.[56]

The religious awakenings that began with the coming of Timothy Dwight to the presidency of Yale College in 1795, rapidly spread through the country in the often spectacular revivals that are known as the Second Great Awakening. Revivalism as institutionalized and conventionalized during this period was an incarnation in the religious life of the nation of the general pietistic movement with its thrust to internalize (or in Luckmann's terms, to "privatize") religious experience.[57]

Two fairly recent studies of the Second Great Awakening come essentially to the same conclusion in this respect. Ralph E. Morrow concluded that "the Great Revival was a gigantic exhibition of privatism in religion" for the leaders, "against the view that the church spoke to man in all his relationships . . . put the practice of promoting personal piety," and this "thrust of 'primitive' and 'apostolic' religion cut between church and society and hardened distinctions between them that impoverished both.''[58]

Similarly Richard D. Birdsall in his study of ''The Second Great Awakening and the New England Social Order,'' concluded that ''the core'' of the movement ''was in the area of individual belief'' for ''instead of the strenuous aim of the original Puritanism to Christianize the social order, there would be an effort to Christianize the hearts of men and to convert the heathen.''[59]

But while the Second Great Awakening was a gigantic exhibition of the privatization of religion, it was also a massive orthodox counter-revolution against the ''new religion'' (Crane Brinton's ''Enlightenment with a capital E'') which had provided the theological legitimation for the constitutional and legal structure of ''the first new nation,'' and for participation in the social and political life of the commonwealth.[60] The orthodox leaders of this counter-revolution turned back to fossilized pre-seventeenth century theologies for the premises and structure of their intellectual lives, and with only slight concessions to the main currents of modern thought, sought to repristinate and maintain the theological perspective of old Christendom.

Thus, as the colonial revivals drove a wedge between ''salvation'' and the fate of society, the long-time effect of the Second Great Awakening was so to split them apart in the United States that when, a century later, Walter Rauschenbusch somewhat timidly suggested that there was a ''relation between Christianity and the social crisis''[61] of his day, the idea seemed utterly alien to a majority of the nation's clergy and laity. And when in September 1935 an editor of the self-consciously prestigious *The Christian Century* sought to explain "Why No Revival" as was expected during the depression, he suggested as obvious that the evangelical churches had contributed to the lack of belief in seeking "help from God" by stressing that religion "has nothing inherently to do with these social and economic matters." Therefore, he concluded, the "Christian church has come into this depression wholly unprepared to take account of it, and to minister to the deepest human need which it discloses."[62]

Truly, the eggs laid by the colonial revivalists had come home to roost.

Meanwhile there has been the eighteenth century, and the eighteenth century means the Rights of Man, Republicanism, and Revolution.

WILLARD L. SPERRY, 1928

And as far as I can see, human life is people. It's even simpler than that. It's Oneself, a simple, separate person. But Oneself exists by virtue of a world shared with other selves. Our life is the intersection of the Self with an Other. In the intense personal form this intersection is love, and in the ideal, general form it's the Republic. Jesus gave us the moral shape of this Republic— the Sign of the Cross.

ROSS LOCKRIDGE, JR., *Raintree County*

III

Christendom, Enlightenment, and Revolution

I have indicated that as I conceive the study of religion in American history, the basic interpretative motif is experience. It means that one is to try to account for the peculiarities of a particular institution that give it its distinctive character by noting the unique *experiences* of that institution compared with the commonly shared experiences of the community of which it is a part.

That Christianity has assumed a distinctive shape in the United States seems obvious.[1] I suggest that the peculiarities that make it distinctive are the result of the necessity in a relatively brief time to accommodate[2] the old Christianity to a strange new environment in which social and geographical space, and social and political revolution were most prominent.

But it was the experience of the religion of Christendom with religious pluralism defended by civil authority that required revolutionary intellectual and institutional adjustments. By pluralism I mean here a multiplicity of organized religious groups in the commonwealth. Each species of the genus Christian achieves distinctive identity and reason for independent being by its peculiar emphasis on one or more of the doctrines shared by all. In the strange chorus of the Christian denominations in the United States they all sing the same song but with different tunes.

The internalization of religion in the eighteenth century (noted in Chapter II) with consequent separation of "salvation" from responsibility for the instituted structures of their society, enabled Christians to accept pluralism and religious freedom without feeling a necessity to come to terms with it theologically. They were not inclined to look this gift horse in the mouth. Had they done so they might have discovered that it was a Trojan horse in the Christian citadel. Christians should have learned to be wary of gifts bearing Greeks.

In our pluralistic society, if one presumes to talk about "religion" a decent respect for his listeners requires that he try to make clear what *he* has in mind.

"Religion" is a subject formally dealt with in almost every university discipline, and naturally spoken of in each in the particular dialect of the tribe. Because we recognize concepts by the words they usually come clothed in, specialists often find it difficult to recognize even one of their own favorite concepts when it is disguised in the terminology of another academic ghetto.[3] Therefore the primary purpose of attempting to define "religion" is to ask whether perhaps a consensus of understanding what we are talking about is concealed by the many different guises in which the concept appears. It seems to me that such a consensus exists, or is emerging.

In 1835 Alexis de Tocqueville, that aboriginal Delphic oracle of things American, noted that no societies have ever managed without general acceptance by the people of some "dogmatic beliefs, that is to say, opinions which men take on trust without discussion." Without such beliefs, "no common action would be possible, and . . . there could be no body social." If society is to exist "it is essential that all the minds of the citizens" be "held together by some leading ideas; and that could never happen unless each of them sometimes came to draw his opinions from the same source and was ready to accept some beliefs ready made."[4]

Tocqueville's view has become a commonplace, enabling Robert Bellah in presenting his view of "American Civil Religion" to note that

> It is one of the oldest of sociological generalizations that any coherent and viable society rests on a common set of moral understandings about good and bad, right and wrong, in the realm of individual and social action. It is almost as widely held that these common moral understandings must also in turn rest upon a common set of religious understandings that provide a picture of the universe in terms of which the moral understandings make sense.[5]

James Baldwin, in a 1959 essay entitled "The Discovery of What It Means to be an American" says he went to Paris to live because he thought he "hated America." But in the experience of living there and trying to relate his experience to "that of others, Negroes and whites, writers and non-writers, I proved, to my astonishment, to be as American as any Texas G.I. And I found my experience was shared by every American writer I knew in Paris." Generalizing from this experience, Mr. Baldwin concluded that "Every society is really governed by hidden laws, by unspoken but profound assumptions on the part of the people. . . ." With this insight, he says, "I was released from the illusion that I hated America" and "I was able to accept my role—as distinguished, I must say, from my 'place'—in the extraordinary drama which is America."[6]

Historian Ralph Henry Gabriel rested his delineation of *The Course of American Democratic Thought* on a concept of shared "social beliefs" that emerged by around 1815, serving Americans "as guides to action, as standards by which to judge the quality of social life, and as goals to inspire humane living." This "cluster of ideas and ideals . . . taken together, made up a national faith which, although unrecognized as such, had the power of a state religion."[7] Gabriel concluded that only by understanding this "faith" or "religion" was it possible to understand the middle period of American history.

Anthropologist Ruth Benedict in her now classic *Patterns of Culture* argued that "What really binds men together" in communities "is their culture,—the ideas and the standards they have in common.''[8] It is these shared beliefs that give them a sense of belonging together and of being different from the peoples of other cultures. To understand a people we must know what those ''ideas and standards'' are.

Edward Shils, writing on ''intellectuals,'' indicated that he assumed that ''actual communities [are] bound together by the acceptance of a common body of standards.''[9] To him we shall return in another connection.

Sociologists, as the quotation from Bellah suggests, have been quick to call the shared ideas and standards ''religious.'' To Robin M. Williams, Jr., ''religion'' is that '' 'system of beliefs' that defines the norms for behavior in the society'' and ''represents a complex of ultimate value-orientations.'' It follows that ''every functioning society has . . . a common religion . . . a common set of ideas, rituals, and symbols'' which supply and/or celebrate ''an over-arching sense of unity. . . .'' It follows that ''no society can be understood without also understanding its religion.''[10] Seen in this context exclusive concentration on describing a people's ''way of life'' as exhibited in their behavior is to miss the primary important thing—what holds them together in a community.

Paul Tillich expressed the same view in more abstract jargon, as befits a theologian:

Religion as ultimate concern is the meaning-giving substance of culture, and culture is the totality of forms in which the basic concern of religion expresses itself. In abbreviations: religion is the substance of culture, culture is the form of religion. Such a consideration definitely prevents the establishment of a dualism of religion and culture.[11]

And, finally, Philip Selznick's one-sentence summary: "A democracy is a normative system in which behavior and belonging are judged on the basis of conformity or lack of it, with the master ideal" shared by the people.[12]

These examples, I trust, are enough to suggest a consensus that the word *religion* is to point to a constellation of shared beliefs respecting the nature of the universe and man's place in it, from which the standards for conduct are supposedly deduced. In this view, *when we speak of the "religion" of an individual or of a community we mean to point to whatever constellation of ideas and standards does in fact give cosmic significance and hence purpose to his or its way of life.*[13]

While some of the ideas and beliefs here referred to may be clearly articulated, more commonly they are of the nature of Tocqueville's "opinions which men take on trust without discussion," that is, assume or presuppose. In philosopher A. N. Whitehead's words, "Religion has been and is now the major source of those ideals which add to life a sense of purpose that is worthwhile." It follows, he added, that "apart from religion, expressed in ways generally intelligible, populations sink into the apathetic task of daily survival, with minor alleviations."[14] In that case, for example, "national security" becomes the ultimate goal that guides national policies.

I wish to emphasize three implications of this consensus definition of "religion": (1) that the religion of a society is whatever system of beliefs that does actually provide cosmic legitimation for its institutions, and the activities of its people; (2) that every individual, every community, has his or its religion; and (3) that the central content of the "religion" is what is assumed or presupposed by most believers, that is, has to do with what to them is obvious. Hence Baldwin's reference to the "hidden laws" that govern society. For nothing is more hidden from most persons than the presuppositions[15] on which their whole structure of thinking rests.[16]

However, at least a few reflective individuals in every society *are* conscious of the fact that they hold some "truths to be self-evident"—persons who realize with Franklin that there are some things they have "never doubted." These are the "intellectuals," and, as Shils says, "There would be intellectuals in society even if there were no intellectuals by disposition."[17] Baldwin concluded that their calling was to make others aware of these "hidden laws" that determine their thinking and acting.

If we presume to talk about "religion" in our pluralistic society we must realize that the word points to a numerous family in which there are hundreds of genera (the world's religions) and thousands of species and sub-species (e.g., denominations) each with its own protective institutional shell.[18] In such a society one cannot be overtly and socially "religious" without choosing to associate with one of the thousand or more vigorously competitive species. Such competition tends to induce the members of each species to claim, implicitly at least, to be the only true representatives of the family. I call this the "Parson Thwackum syndrome," for that cleric in Henry Fielding's *History of Tom Jones* stated the position most lucidly. "When I mention religion," he said, "I mean the Christian religion; and not only the Christian religion, but the Protestant religion; and not only the Protestant religion, but the Church of England."[19] Thus to Thwackum, Anglican, Protestant, Christian, and Religion were synonymous. The Thwackums among us erase all distinction between family, genus, species, and subspecies of religion. And the Thwackum perspective is not uncommon even among the very learned and sophisticated professors in the prestige theological schools who confuse their beliefs with *the* "authentic faith." Ruth Benedict, recognizing the syndrome, warned "white culture" against its tendency "always to identify our own local ways of behaving with behavior, or our own socialized habits with Human Nature," and, she might have added, our species of religion with "religion."[20]

Further, a genus or species of religion may be defined and defended from two quite different points of view— from that of the insider and from that of an outsider. To the insider, talk and writing about his species of religion is analogous to autobiography. To the outsider, talk about a species of religion is analogous to biography, the voice of knowledge about.[21] In sophisticated dress this distinction was invoked by H. Richard Niebuhr in his *The Meaning of Revelation.*[22] His use of the terms "inner" and "outer" history has been widely adopted by those who gain a reputation for profound thought by repeating the terminology of a Master.

Down through the centuries of Christendom able theologians nourished the belief that there was an absolute and eternal difference in kind between the "natural" unregenerate persons (the outsiders) and the regenerate "saints" (the insiders). Jonathan Edwards, certainly one of the best and the brightest, etched the line between them with great clarity—arguing that "natural men" could no more understand the "gracious influences which the saints are subjects of" than the person with no sense of taste whatever could apprehend "the sweet taste of honey . . . by only looking on it, and feeling of it."[23] In this obscurantist citadel of euphoric and absolute assurance, generations of Christians have smugly found an impregnable defense of their peculiar species of Christianity.

More surprising to me, in 1962 Professor Arthur S. Link applied this distinction to the writing of "secular" history in the twentieth century. Assuming that the historian "is called to be a mere chronicler of the past," he argued that the non-Christian historian's chronicle is subject to "the tyranny of the ego's insatiable demands for its own understanding and control of history." But God gives Christians "the ability to be good and faithful historians" through the gift of the Spirit. Therefore the Christian's history, being "purged of the ego's distortions and perversions," is the only truly "objective" chronicle. Mr. Link concluded that "if the writers of the Biblical record were 'inspired,' that is, given grace to be true historians, then we, too, can be 'inspired' even as we are justified."[24] Readers of Mr. Link's writings will hereafter note that the author modestly intimates that they belong in the canon of inspired pronouncements.

From the standpoint of those of us who live outside the temples in which such grace-endowed fellows dwell, what "religion" is can be only an opinion based on inferences drawn from observation and analysis of what self-styled "religious" people do and say, individually and collectively, and of their explanation and defense of their saying and doing. For as John Dewey noted, we cannot observe religion-in-general, but only genera and species of the family.[25]

This is to say that outsiders, for whom religion is as religion does, can produce only biographies of the species or genera of "religion." And if Jonathan Edwards was, and if Arthur S. Link is, right, the communication gulf between insiders and outsiders is impassable. To the outsider the insider's autobiographical argument is unconvincing or meaningless because he lives in a different world of reality in which the insider's claim is an obscurantist refuge for all the species of privatized religiosity. Ruth Benedict delineated the contrast between the two perspectives, as only an outsider could do, in her contrast between open and closed groups. "The distinction between any closed group and outside peoples," she wrote,

> becomes in terms of religion that between the true believers and the heathen. Between these two categories for thousands of years there were no common meeting-points. No ideas or institutions that held in the one were valid in the other. Rather all institutions were seen in opposing terms according as they belonged to one or the other of the very often slightly differentiated religions: on the one side it was a question of Divine Truth and the true believer, of revelation and of God; on the other it was a matter of

moral error, of fables, of the damned and of devils. There could be no question of equating the attitudes of the opposed groups and hence no question of understanding from objectively studied data the nature of this important human trait, religion.[26]

I have argued that the experience of the old Christianity in the New World resulted in the internalizing of Christianity with the consequent separation in principle of one's "salvation" from the sense of responsibility for the social, economic, and political life of his society. The nature of this separation can also be delineated in contemporary sociological language, and my interest in consensus induces me to try to do so.

Talcott Parsons is, I take it, a respectable representative of the discipline that has sometimes aspired to be crowned the modern Queen of the Sciences. Parsons distinguishes between "cultural systems" and "social systems," and describes the relation between them. "Social systems," he says, "are organized about the exigencies of interaction among acting units, both individual persons and collective units." In analyzing them we merely describe "what in fact is done" or predict "what will be."[27]

On the other hand, "Cultural systems . . . are organized about the patterning of meaning in symbolic systems ["meaning systems"]."[28] As for the relation between them, "meaning systems are always in some respects and to some degree normative in their significance" for action and interaction in the social system. Or, as I would say, the "meaning system" provides cosmic legitimation for the "social system."

Parsons continues: the function of the "meaning system" is that it specifies "what in some sense *should* be done and evaluate[s] the actual performance accordingly . . . ,'' that is, because it defines what is normal behavior, and is internalized, it stands in judgment over deviant action. This all seems in keeping with the complex definition of "religion" I spelled out above. To me, functionally Parsons' "meaning system" *is* the religion of the society.

In applying this definition to an understanding of our America, it is natural to suppose that the religion (meaning system) that legitimates its social, political, and economic system is that Christianity given institutionalized form in the many denominations. This I have come to believe is a mistake. My thesis, that the internalization of religion beginning with the eighteenth-century revivals effectively separated assurance of salvation from a sense of responsibility for the institutions of the convert's society, means just that.[29] This is to say that the species of religion incarnated in the denominations with their massive institutional inertia, is not the religion that actually sets and legitimates the norms of our society—that the theology of the denominations does not legitimate the political and legal structure of the commonwealth.[30]

It follows that it is not very profitable to go looking for the real theology of our Republic in the dusty historical attics of the institutionalized piosity of our contemporary society. Certainly it is not profitable to look only there. Recognition of this separation was always implicit, for example, in those educators who, while holding that the public schools inculcated the moral and spiritual values of the democracy, were very careful to divorce those values from all species of the religion institutionalized in the nation's sects.

I assume that the general health and well-being of a commonwealth-society hinges upon a harmony between its meaning and social systems—between its religion and its society—that the theology inculcated by the society's dominant "churches" suggests the cosmic significance of the norms that are invoked to control behavior in the social, economic, political and judicial spheres. This is to say that religion is the mainspring of an integrated society. When the mainspring is broken the society runs down. Or, as Alfred North Whitehead expressed it,

> Religion has been and is now the major source of those ideals which add to life a sense of purpose that is worth while. Apart from religion, expressed in ways generally intelligible, populations sink into the apathetic task of daily survival, with minor alleviations.[31]

That the mainspring of the old-line denominations in America is broken, seems widely assumed today, and even persuasively documented.[32] A few years ago it was exuberantly self-confessed by professors in jet-set theological schools who joined Friedrich Nietzsche's madman in the secular city's marketplace (for example, in *Time* magazine) proclaiming the death of God. More recently representatives of these self-liquidating theologians have intimated, with more than usual insight, that it is their theology that is dead, or at least like the sheep of Little Bo-Peep, is lost and they do not know where to find it.[33]

I am willing to take their word for it. But the loss of their ideology does not perturb me insofar as the welfare of the Republic is concerned. For I hold that *their* lost theology is not nor ever has been the mainspring of that Republic—that *the* theology of the Republic is that of "Enlightenment" in Crane Brinton's sense. And it is not clear that this mainspring is broken. Indeed Michael Novak was easily able to develop a persuasive argument that it is very much alive; that, indeed, "the tradition in which intellectuals ordinarily define themselves [today] is that of the Enlightenment,"—that Enlightenment is "the dominant religion" in contemporary society.[34] And Martin E. Marty, defender of an implicit but vaguely defined Protestant orthodoxy against "religion in general," has argued that in American history, "while Protestants pointed with pride to their achievements they hardly realized that the typically rationalist view of the irrelevancy of theological distinctions in a pluralist society was pulling the rug out from under them." And this means, Marty concluded, borrowing a punch line from Oscar Handlin, "that the Enlightenment prevailed over 'the forms American religion took in its development from Calvinism.' "[35] That most of us are closer to the tradition of "Enlightenment" than to eighteenth-century Christian orthodoxy we realize when we stop to think that we would no doubt find Franklin, Jefferson, Madison, even Thomas Paine more congenial dinner company than Jonathan Edwards, Samuel Davies, George Whitefield, or Timothy Dwight.

Mr. Marty's thesis, noted above, suggests that one might say of most academic theology in America what George Herbert Mead said of Josiah Royce's philosophy, that it "was part of the escape from the crudity of American life, not an interpretation of it," for "it . . . did not root in the active life of the community" and

therefore "was not an interpretation of American life."
So, G. H. Mead continued, although from around 1800
"culture was sought vividly in institutions of learning,
in lyceums and clubs, it did not reflect the political and
economic activities which were fundamental in American life."[36]

And one might say of Marty's Protestant Christians,
unaware that the rug was being pulled out from under
them by "Enlightenment," what G. H. Mead said of
William James: "He was not aware of the break
between the profound processes of American life [Par-
sons' "social system"] and its culture [Parsons' "culture system"]."[37]

In a most perceptive essay published in 1964, the
late historian-theologian Joseph Haroutunian gave
more definite theological content to the development
to which Marty and G. H. Mead pointed. The predominant Christian orthodoxy in the United States, he
argued, "has been a *tour de force,* which has persisted
and flourished largely either as a denial of or as an
escape from American experience." He specified

> Its supernaturalism and appeal to authority; its
> pitching of Christian doctrine against the ideas of the
> scientific community and its advocacy of faith as
> against intelligence; its severing prayer from work
> and the sacred from the secular have made orthodoxy
> an alien spirit in American life and its theology an
> alien mind in a land which has rewarded industry
> and method with good things and common pros-
> perity.[38]

After giving due regard to the liberal and other
theological movements in the United States he summarized his view in an understatement: "It appears

that American Christianity has done less than justice to American Experience, and so have American theologians.''

I assume that the theologians are the intellectuals of a community of faith or belief. I am using the word *intellectual(s)* in the sense developed by Shils and Parsons in the articles noted above.

In Parsons' terminology, the intellectual is ''expected . . . to put cultural considerations above social,'' his function being to define and, presumably, to articulate and disseminate the ''meaning system'' (or ''value orientation'') of his society.

Shils spelled this out in clearer fashion. He assumed, as noted above, that communities are ''bound together by the acceptance of a common body of standards'' which are internalized and ''continually . . . applied by each member in his own work and in the institutions which assess and select works and persons for appreciation or condemnation.'' These standards are seldom rationalized and made overt but are carried and maintained primarily in ''songs, histories, poems, biographies, and constitutions, etc., which diffuse a sense of affinity among the members of the society.''

Intellectuals are driven by a ''need to penetrate beyond the screen of immediate concrete experience'' —that is, beyond the concerns relative to Parsons' ''social system''—to the ''ultimate principles'' implicit therein, which is to define ''the existing body of cultural values.'' Then by ''preaching, teaching, and writing'' in ''schools, churches, newspapers, and similar structures'' they ''infuse into sections of the population which are intellectual neither by inner vocation nor by social role, a perceptiveness and an imagery

which they would otherwise lack.''[39] Here in Shils'
terminology we may recognize James Baldwin's conception of the responsibility of the artist-writer to clarify
and articulate the ''hidden-laws'' that govern his society and himself.

I hear Parsons and Shils saying that the task of the
intellectuals is to infuse in the population the ''beliefs
and standards'' that define what is normal behavior in
their society, and that these are legitimated by the
''ultimate principles implicit'' in them. This means in
my way of speaking that ideally intellectuals would
assume responsibility for inculcating the ''religion'' of
their community.

This seems to me essentially the thesis David W.
Noble developed in his book, *Historians Against History: The Frontier Thesis and the National Covenant in
American Historical Writing Since 1890*. The historian,
Noble argues, ''is our most important secular theologian,'' responsible for describing and defending the
covenant that makes us a people, being always ready
both to ''explain how his country has achieved its
uniqueness'' and to ''warn against the intrusion of
alien influences.''[40]

What I have described as the separation of ''salvation'' from social responsibility, in the terminology of
Parsons and Shils could be described as a separation of
the ''cultural system'' and value orientation professed
in a community from the actual ''social system,'' or the
divorce of ''religion from what G. H. Mead called ''the
political and economic activities which were fundamental in American life.''

Traditionally in Christendom ''the Church,'' a very
tangible institution *in*, but conceived as not entirely *of*,

the society,[41] was the home of the intellectuals. The Church in this respect was roughly analogous to the University in our society. For those who lived during the centuries of Catholic Christendom, as for the Puritans of early Massachusetts Bay, theologians played the role in society that Parsons and Shils designate as *the* role of intellectuals in any society.[42] Further, they were expected to give guidance to rulers and people, in minute detail if necessary, for they were the recognized interpreters of the proper application of the general standards to specific issues. In this social-cultural structure "salvation" was inextricably bound to right conduct in every area of life from birth to last rites.

With the fragmentation of the transnational Church by the Reformation, and the establishment of religious pluralism, this unified authoritarian structure was destroyed, and Christianity was thereafter incarnated in many different and highly competitive institutions, each legitimated by its absolutized parochial interpretation of the common "Gospel." Each Established church that resulted made for its place in its nation the same sort of claims that the universal Catholic church had made for its ubiquitous transnational authority. In other words, the new nations reverted to tribalism, and an Established church was the institutionalization of the nation's tribal cult.

In this situation no substantive difference was made between "Church" and "commonwealth." They were merely two ways of looking at the same body of people. This was evidenced in the legal structure by the merging of monarch into God, legitimated by some forms of the doctrine of the divine right of kings.[43] In this context the role of the theologian of an Established church was that of a true intellectual of and for his nation-society.

When the American Revolution was completed, let us say with John Adams by around 1815,[44] not only had the Established Church of England been rejected, but, more important, the very idea of "Establishment" had been discarded in principle by the new Constitution. For the first time in Christendom there was legal *religious freedom* as distinct from toleration in a commonwealth.[45] Church and state could no longer be seen as coextensive functional institutionalized authorities— as merely two ways of looking at the same society. A church became a voluntary association within the commonwealth, in competition with perhaps hundreds of others. Loyalty to God, symbol of the highest ideals and standards ("cultural system") could now be distinguished from loyalty to monarch or state, symbols of nation ("social system"), and it was possible to conceive that the two might be in conflict. This development is what John Adams meant by "the Revolution" —the change that took place "in the minds and hearts of the people" which he described as "a change in their religious sentiments of their duties and obligations."[46]

With this Revolution the theologian, who had lost his transnational perspective with the Reformation, lost also his national perspective, and became the intellectual for but one of the multitude of competing sects. Now his primary role was to construct a solid defense of his sect's peculiar species of Christianity against all the other sects making the same absolutistic claim. Because the one thing all Christians held in common was the authority of Scripture, all such defenses were erected on this foundation. This meant that even while ostensibly defending the authority of the Bible against sceptics, infidels and atheists, each sect was actually contending against all other Christian groups for sole possession of the revelation by right of having the only, or most nearly, correct interpretation of it. Meantime the Revolution meant that all their sectarian claims had been made completely irrelevant to the individual's status and rights as a citizen, and to the being and well-being of the commonwealth in which they lived. Thus the competition between the sects undermined belief in the distinctive beliefs of all of them. For in the minds of Mr. and Ms. John Q. Public the strident claims of the sects simply cancelled each other out, as their Republic was teaching them that no sect's distinctiveness had a bearing on their rights as citizens.[47]

Meantime the new kind of commonwealth that had emerged in Christendom found cosmic legitimation in "Enlightenment" theology—the cosmopolitan perspective that induced Benjamin Franklin to pray that God would "grant, that not only the Love of Liberty, but a thorough Knowledge of the Rights of Man, may pervade all the Nations of the Earth, so that a Philosopher may set his Foot anywhere on its Surface, and say, 'This is my Country.'"[48] The same sentiment prompted Alexander Hamilton to suggest in the first Federalist Paper that in the new kind of nation being born philanthropy (love for mankind) must always temper patriotism (love for country), which is to say that "national security" is not necessarily always the ultimate consideration.

It was this cosmopolitan theology that the Christian denominations almost universally rejected during the course of the revivals that swept across the nation following the 1790s. In doing so they turned back to pre-eighteenth century theologians, or to the theologians of Europe's Established churches, for the framework of their intellectual structures, while the "meaning system" that informed and legitimated the social, economic, political and judicial systems of the nation followed in the tradition of "Enlightenment" thinking.[49] It was this development that institutionalized the separation of "salvation" from the convert's responsibility for the structures of his society.[50]

One of the most extensively documented historical generalizations is that "Enlightenment" was driven underground by social opprobrium and character assassination of the "infidel," but that its "meaning system" (to use Parsons' terms) was never examined for its intellectual merits and refuted by Christian theologians.[51]

The "Enlightenment" meaning system continued, of course, to have its more or less able defenders. But most of them might rightly complain with Thomas Paine that his Christian opponents confounded "a dispute about authenticity with a dispute about doctrines," that is, in answer to his questioning of the authority of the Bible as sole revelation of God for teaching man his duty, they quoted Scripture to refute him.[52] This suggests what I suspect was the case, that the great majority of clerical leaders and theologians did not recognize the real issue or realize the nature of the revolution in thinking that was taking place. Each in his denominational stockade tended to absolutize and universalize his parochial species of Christianity, while sharing with those in his Christian opponents' ghettos the common abhorrence of "infidelity." The "infidel" was on everyone's enemies list.[53]

This meant, to repeat my thesis, that every ardent defense of sectarian Christianity, however unintentional, was by implication an attack on the mainspring of the Republic.[54] Consequently the intellectuals—the unofficial "theologians" of the Republic—explaining, defending, acting upon, and infusing the values of the commonwealth were commonly anathema to the leaders of institutionalized Christianity, or, as by Robert Baird who published his *Religion in America* in 1844–45, were posthumously metamorphosed into his species of good sectarian Christians.[55]

This development meant the emergence in the commonwealth of two disparate, even competing "culture systems," inculcating different conceptions of a proper "social system," each with its own kind of "intellectuals." Many theologians of the sects continued to talk as if they were the exponents of the normative "culture system" of the commonwealth, while actually they represented only that of, at best Christianity in general, at worst their exclusive sect. Meantime the intellectuals of the commonwealth, as e.g., Jefferson, Franklin, Lincoln, and even Eisenhower, naturally found no real religious home in any existing sect. And many sensitive persons squirmed to have the best of both worlds, usually ending by giving each a separate but equal compartment in their minds—like those Lutherans I noted in Chapter II.[56]

The question of the place of sectarian theologians in the commonwealth was solved by default. For with the general erosion of belief noted above, they lost even their vocation as defenders of what the Parson Thwackums among them have called denominational distinctives against both those of the other Christian sects and unbelievers. They became at their best defenders of the theologically amorphous but highly moralistic species of Christianity-in-general represented in recent decades by *The Christian Century,* at their worst pugnacious and powerful sectarian isolationists like the Rev. Carl McIntire. In either case, having usually been pro-grammed in their theological schools to confuse the cosmopolitan ''Enlightenment'' theology with worship of the state, they have found it hard to find a plausibly significant role to play in the society.[57] George Santayana described the fanatic as one who redoubles his efforts when he has lost his aim. This is an apt characterization of the faddishness that has characterized professional theology during the past several decades.[58]

It is not surprising, when seen in this context, that as long ago as 1933, theological school professor John C. Bennett lamented a widespread ''feeling of theological homelessness'' among his kind.[59]

. . . atheism, irreligion, or licentiousness . . . have no right by any
law in the United States to . . . propagate opinions and proselytize.
ROBERT BAIRD, 1845

Mr. Jefferson . . . brought in modes of thought . . . which are . . .
bitterly pernicious [and] can only operate . . . destructively; working
as a . . . latent poison against all government . . . [The Declaration
is an] atheistic bill.
HORACE BUSHNELL, 1861, 1864

. . . supercelestial thoughts, Montaigne notes sardonically, tend
to go hand in hand with subterranean conduct.
DONALD M. FRAME, translator,
The Complete Essays of Montaigne

IV

*Christendom's Orthodoxies vs.
the Premises of the Republic*

The discipline of history is devoted to suggesting
answers to a question, the archetype of which is, ''How
did they, or we, get that way?''

In the past three chapters I have delineated what
seem to me some plausible historical explanations of
''how we got that way.''

I have suggested that when seen in the perspective of
what prevailed universally in Christendom for fourteen
centuries there are three strikingly unusual things about
the religious scene in the United States: (1) the religious
pluralism upheld by the civil authority in a nation;

(2) the widespread belief that religion has nothing to do with the political and economic institutions of the society; and (3) the theologically bifurcated minds of many church members.

Here I intend to focus on the third—the tension in the minds and hearts of many Americans between fundamental principles of their inherited traditional Christian orthodoxy and fundamental premises of the Republic in which they live. This is the unresolved theological problem that lies at the heart not only of our religious establishment but of our whole culture.[1]

I have noted my agreement with Crane Brinton that during the seventeenth and eighteenth centuries there emerged in Christendom "a new religion"[2] that for the first time offered the people of a Christian nation an alternative to orthodox Christianity.

That new religion had a definite theological content that differed in important respects, and still differs, from Christian orthodoxy.[3] But even learned Christian insiders have seldom noted this, and when they did they have been apt to accentuate only negative differences from their orthodoxy.

Typical is Professor Winthrop Hudson's treatment wherein, after summarizing its doctrinal elements, he adds,

> The most noteworthy feature of this Deist "creed" was its omissions. There was nothing distinctively Christian about it—no mention of any special work of Christ, of man's sinful nature and consequent need of redemption, or of any necessary dependence upon Biblical revelation.[4]

This is very much in the Parson Thwackum tradition, the impression it conveys being that because it is not "distinctively Christian" according to the species of Christianity Mr. Hudson had in mind, that therefore it is not authentically "religious" at all. Hudson's typical insider's assessment of an outsider's perspective reminds me of the mythical male chauvinist curmudgeon who declared that the most noteworthy feature of his wife was a deplorable omission, so there was nothing distinctively male about her.[5]

An outsider is more inclined to accentuate the positive—to stress the constellation of positive doctrines that made up the "Enlightenment" creed, and to wonder that the deist believed what in our twentieth century might well get him typed as no better than a "fundamentalist" in a majority of our snobbishly "liberal" middle-class churches.

"Enlightenment" (in Crane Brinton's sense) is more aptly described positively as a radical monotheism, or, as one might well characterize Jefferson's position, a Unitarianism of the First Person—Thomas Paine's "plain, pure, and unmixed belief of one God."[6]

"God" for these men was an unquestioned presupposition, not a problem as He has become for many professional theologians today. Whatever else they may have been they were not atheists.[7] They were "infidels" in the precise sense the term then conveyed, in that they rejected the orthodox Christian premises: that the Bible was the only revelation of God to man, and that Jesus was Deity.

The foundation of their perspective was that other strand in the Christian tradition—the concept of God's second volume of revelation, the Creation. Yes, said Thomas Paine, "there is a word of God; there is a revelation. The WORD OF GOD IS THE CREATION WE BEHOLD; and it is in *this word,* . . . that God

speaketh universally to man" and "reveals to man all
that is necessary for man to know of God."[8] John
Adams in 1813 was even more rhapsodic:

> The human Understanding is a revelation from its
> Maker which can never be disputed or doubted.
> There can be no Scepticism, Phrrhonism or Incredul-
> ity or Infidelity here. No Prophecies, no Miracles are
> necessary to prove this celestial communication.[9]

Where the orthodox argued that *some* persons were
enabled by grace to understand the revelation in
Scripture, the intellectuals of "Enlightenment" held
that all men are gifted by their Creator with "Reason"
or Adams' "Understanding," that enabled them to
read and understand the revelation in His creation
which, Paine argued, "no human invention can coun-
terfeit or alter."

Both those of orthodox and "Enlightenment" persuasion agreed that man's duty was to obey the will of
God, and that he learned what God's will was by
interpreting God's revelation. They disagreed on the
locus and nature of that revelation, and on what
enabled finite humans to read and understand it. As
William McLoughlin so aptly put the distinction, for
Isaac Backus "truth came through the heart by grace
while for Jefferson it came . . . through the head by
reason."[10] Christian orthodoxy was exclusivistic. "Enlightenment" was inclusivistic.

The obverse side of the high doctrine of God as
Creator and Governor of the universe was the finite
limitation of the creature, man, *in every respect*. This
meant that finite man could not have absolute assurance of final knowledge of anything, even of the

existence of God and his own salvation. All mankind could have was "opinions," and these, James Madison explained, depend solely "on the evidence contemplated in their own minds."[11] It followed that opinions could neither be borrowed from others nor imposed by coercion. Granted this conception of the creature's limitations, and two things follow: that freedom of religion, speech, press, etc., are "unalienable" rights, and that man is not "saved" by knowledge and must live by faith in the Creator and His Providence.

Madison made this clear in the *Memorial and Remonstrance on the Religious Rights of Man* (1784) in which he defined religion as one's *opinion* of the "duty which we owe to our creator, and the manner of discharging it." Opinions cannot be directed by force but "only by reason and conviction." Therefore every man's religion "must be left to the conviction and conscience of every man." This is to say that freedom of religion is an "unalienable right," that is a responsibility that the individual cannot delegate.[12] Religion, being an opinion, "cannot follow the dictates of other men."

Not questioning the existence of the Deity, it followed that the individual's duty was "to render the creator such homage and such only, as he believes to be acceptable to him"—a neat way of stating and legitimating the principle of the right of private judgment.

One's duty to the creator, Madison continued, "is precedent, both in order of time and degree of obligation, to the claims of civil society" because "before any man can be considered as a member of civil society, he must be considered as a subject of the governor of the universe." It follows that when any person swears his

allegiance to "any particular civil society" he does it
*"with the saving his allegiance to the universal
sovereign."* This was a nice way of saying that "We
must obey God rather than men" (Acts 5:29), and
would seem to be enough to lay to rest the popular
view that "Enlightenment" religion is worship of the
State. Madison categorically rejected idolatry of any
human forms, most emphatically that of the State.

Central in this perspective was the ability to separate
conceptually religiosity as feeling, experience, and ideas
from the institutional forms in and by which it was
made tangible in society. John Adams clearly exemplified this when he wrote to Thomas Jefferson in January
1825:

> The substance and essence of Christianity as I under-
> stand it is eternal and unchangeable and will bear
> examination forever but it has been mixed with
> extraneous ingredients which I think will not bear
> examination and they ought to be separated.[13]

To men of this perspective the "substance and
essence of Christianity" was the same as that of all
other genera of religion. This was expressed in the
concept of "the essentials of every religion"—the
dogmas Franklin said he "never doubted." On this
anti-Thwackum model one might, as Franklin, recognize the many institutional manifestations of the essentials and yet maintain his belief in the absolute Creator
and Governor of the universe, which belief guarded
them against the maelstrom of simple relativism.

The institutionalized forms[14] of religion being merely
the humanly contrived vehicles for the conveyance of
the essentials, were subject to judgment, primarily on

the basis of their practical moral efficacy. So Franklin, assuming that the essentials were "to be found in all the religions we had in our country," said that he "respected them all, Tho' with different degrees of respect, as I found them . . . mix'd with other articles, which without any tendency to inspire, promote, or confirm morality, serv'd principally to divide us. . . ." As we have noted above, when Franklin was convinced that the minister's motive was to make good Presbyterians rather than good citizens he shrugged and left the church. For those of this perspective the only justifiable purpose of a religious observance was its inculcation and/or legitimation of virtue (good morals). They could not conceive of religious faith without works[15] and insofar were the sons of that James whom, I have been told, Luther would gladly have thrown out of the canon. They could not conceive of "salvation" apart from exemplification in overt responsibility for the being and continued well-being of their society and commonwealth.

We should be clear that these men were not anti-religious, anti-Christian, or even anti-denominational churches. They represented, as Professor William Warren Sweet argued long ago,[16] a revolt against Established churches in the name of true religion, or as in Jefferson's case, the pure moral teachings of Jesus.[17] Assuming that every denominational church taught and inculcated in its members the "essentials" of every religion, whether they knew it or not and whatever might be the particular forms of their theology and practice, they might say with Jefferson that although there were "various kinds" of religion they were "all good enough; all sufficient to preserve peace and order. . . .''[18] Their hope might be expressed in the words of F.C.S. Schiller, to wit, that ''we may learn to regard our differences [over religion] as unessential, as the bad reasons which those who differ from us give for doing the right thing; and practically this suffices.''[19]

Finally, the whole structure of ''Enlightenment'' rested on unquestioned belief in the Creator and Governor of the universe—the absolute presupposition that enabled Jefferson to assert in the ''Act for Establishing Religious Freedom'' in Virginia

> that truth is great and will prevail if left to herself, that she is the proper and sufficient antagonist to error, and has nothing to fear from the conflict, unless by human interposition disarmed of her natural weapons, free argument and debate, errors ceasing to be dangerous, when it is permitted freely to contradict them.[20]

It followed that the surest pathway to truth was through free conflict of opinions, that, as Jefferson said, ''Difference of opinion is advantageous in religion [because] the several sects perform the office of a *censor morum* over such [*sic*] other.''[21] It was on the basis of this premise that for the first time in Christendom civil authority presumed to protect the right of every religious group freely to propagate its own views openly, as freely to condemn and try to dissuade others from the views of its opponents, and to proselytize their members.

This indeed was hard doctrine for many orthodox establishment Christians of the time who, in keeping with centuries of Christian thinking and practice, assumed the necessity for the use of the sword of steel in defense of their species of Christianity. It was the doctrine against which the majority of Christian leaders set themselves, implicitly or explicitly, during the era of the Second Great Awakening, turning back to what Emerson called the stationary forms of pre-seventeenth century theologies for the structure and sustenance of their intellectual lives. In doing so they surrendered intellectual initiative and relevance to the leaders of the main currents of modern thought which flowed from "Enlightenment."[22]

This massive turning of "attention . . . to the old faith of the fathers"[23] effectively separated the religious from the intellectual life of the society, and the two were duly institutionalized in denominations and universities respectively. Theological education tended thereafter to become training for nourishing organized religious life in the nineteenth and twentieth centuries on the theological premises of the first to the sixteenth centuries while conducting a rearguard action against modern thought.[24] The result is reflected in the remark by Henry Pratt Judson, a scholarly Baptist leader, in 1908, that modern man does not find religion "substantial in its intellectual basis" or effective in its "application to social conditions"—a situation that led, he said, to "a growing concern for the relation of Christianity to European and American civilization."[25]

In previous chapters I have noted that every "sectarian" defense of Christianity may be implicitly at least an attack on the rational foundations of the Republic. I have also called attention to the extensive study that revealed the consequent and typical bifurcation of the minds of Lutheran church members in the

United States—the ability to hold two mutually exclusive theologies in their minds at the same time.

Within this general context of American history there is a strand of definite, self-conscious opposition to the premises of the Republic on the part of some very eminent Christian leaders. This I think ought to be the subject of extensive research in the interests of more adequate understanding of our pluralistic commonwealth. At present I am able only to call attention to three striking examples of such overt opposition.[26]

It was a very complex alignment of forces during the last quarter of the eighteenth century in the English colonies that brought about the declarations for religious freedom that reversed Christian teaching and practice of fourteen centuries standing.[27] The founders faced the practical political problem posed by the fact that existing, albeit unintended, religious pluralism made it obvious that if there was to be a *united* states made up of the diverse colonies, there could be no nationally Established church in the traditional sense. But neither could there be interference with Establishments where they existed in the new states, notably in New England.

Actually the provisions written into the Constitution and First Amendment represent a territorial solution in which, while the federal congress is forbidden to sponsor establishment, the states are left free to continue to do so if they wish. This meant that the question was localized in the states, and hence that many of the religious and political leaders most directly involved in dealing with it were quite parochial. On only one thing did the representatives of all the many different religious groups apparently agree. Each wanted religious freedom for himself, perhaps largely because every denomination sometime, somewhere in some colony had smarted under the status of a dissenting sect. For this reason they could present a united front against a national Establishment.

But their motives for doing so might be quite parochial, their conception of the meaning of religious freedom quite personal, and their understanding of its implications for the conduct of ecclesiastical affairs determined by their very limited and immediate experience. Professor William G. McLoughlin's extensive and intensive studies of Isaac Backus (1724–1806) and the New England Baptists during the eighteenth century make this clear.

Whatever the merits of psychohistory—and even its father, Erik H. Erikson, has tried to disassociate himself from much that has been "done in the name of this term,"[28] it has reminded us again that revolutionary movements sprout when the right kind of individual internalizes a problem that is bugging his society and era.

Isaac Backus was such a person. From the time of his conversion in 1741 to the end of his life in 1806 he struggled "to draw the line between the rights of individual conscience and the compulsory power of the State," but only as the issue was forced upon him as a dissenting Baptist suffering under the establishment laws of Massachusetts.[29] However, McLoughlin makes clear, in wrestling with his immediate and personal problems, Backus "set forth the principles of separation of Church and State which were to predominate in American life until very recently."[30] McLoughlin calls this strand in the American tradition "sectarian" or "evangelical" pietism, and argues persuasively for its independence from those stemming from Roger Williams on the one hand and Jefferson on the other. Backus, he notes, "evolved his principles and wrote his tracts against the New England establishment before he had even heard of Jefferson or Madison," and he did not begin to read Roger Williams' works until February 1773.[31]

There is no simple way to do justice to the nuances of difference between those McLoughlin calls the evangelical separationists and rationalist-humanists. But their significant difference was in their respective views of the kind of commonwealth that was being born. As stated by McLoughlin, Jefferson and Madison envisaged the creation of "a secular state with 'a high wall of separation' to keep religion at bay." These men "explicitly denied that America was or should be a Christian nation," while "Backus and the Baptists wanted to separate Church and State in order to create a truly Christian state"[32]—assuming, as did "most nineteenth-century evangelicals" after them, "that America was not only a Christian nation but a Protestant one."[33] In the Courts this difference appeared in the question whether Christianity was, following English precedent, part of the common law. Jefferson flatly denied this.[34] Evangelicals assumed and affirmed that it was. In my jargon, the Jeffersonians were "outsiders" and the evangelicals were "insiders" with a typical Thwackum syndrome, and with Parson Thwackum's addendum that honor and morals were "dependent upon this religion; and is consistent with and dependent upon no other."

McLoughlin concisely summarizes the results of the dominance of this evangelical perspective:

Few nineteenth-century evangelicals saw any incon-
sistency in supporting laws to enforce the Protestant
Sabbath or prohibition, laws against blasphemy and
profanity, laws against lotteries, gambling, theater-
going, dancing, and, ultimately, against the teaching
of evolution. In recent years staunch neoevangelical
supporters of Separationism have cried out against
the decisions of the Supreme Court preventing Bible
reading and prayer in the public schools.[35]

McLoughlin's conclusion seems obvious: "Certainly
Jefferson would have approved of these Court decisions,
and so would [Roger] Williams. But it seems certain
that Backus would not." For Backus thought a "mil-
lenial dawn was rising . . . upon a Christian state" and
he was happy because "No man can take a seat in our
[Massachusetts] legislature till he solemnly declares, 'I
believe the Christian religion, and have a firm persuasion of its truth.' "[36] During the nineteenth century,
McLoughlin points out, "Evangelical inheritors" of
Backus' viewpoint found it very "easy . . . to ignore the
rights of non-evangelicals (Catholics, Mormons, the
Indians, Atheists, Freemasons) in order to protect the
moral order of a protestant nation."[37]

I assume that there would be general agreement
among informed citizens today that *this* evangelical
Protestant perspective is contrary to the principles and
premises upon which our Republic rests. And this is an
important dimension of what I mean to suggest when I
argue that sectarian defenses of Christianity have always
tended to undermine the citizens' belief in the American democratic premises. This becomes plain in the
work of Robert Baird (1798–1863) who in the middle of
the nineteenth century clearly argued that the "rights
of conscience" cannot be claimed by non-believers.

Baird was a highly educated Presbyterian who, as agent for various Protestant Societies, had traveled widely in and published books about European countries. He was a person of high visibility when in 1843 his *Religion in America; or, An Account of the Origin, Relation to the State, and Present Condition of the Evangelical Churches in the United States, with Notices of the Unevangelical Denominations* was published in Scotland and was reprinted in the United States the following year.[38] Shortly thereafter it appeared in French, German, Swedish, and Dutch translations. The editor of a recent paperback edition rightly claims Baird's book to be "the best historical summary of major denominations and the most judicious assessment of the distinctive features of religious life in the New World" down to the time of its publication.[39] To this I would add that Baird anticipated most of the interpretative motifs that have guided the study of religion in American history ever since.

Writing originally for an European audience, Baird naturally devoted much space to what he called the several denominations' "relation to the state."

To Baird the United States was a "Christian empire," and "the grand means employed by God in preparing a people" to found such an empire "in the New World was the Reformation," during which "the accumulated rubbish of ages" was cleared away and fresh contact made with God's Word" (32). This provided the impetus that necessarily eventuated in the triumph of "the Voluntary Principle" over "the old system" of civil "support of the Christian ministry and worship." And the grand basis of the voluntary system is "perfect religious freedom . . . freedom of conscience for all: for those who believe Christianity to be true, and for those who do not: for those who prefer one form of worship, and for those who prefer another'' (38).

So far so good. But what did Baird mean?

He devotes one of the longest sections in his book (the 58 pages of Book II) to delineation of ''the relations which the State bore in the different colonies to the Church'' (84), and to demonstrating ''the religious character of the early colonists.'' They were, he points out, religious, Christian, overwhelmingly Protestant, and their religion was not ''inoperative'' (83).

But this argument prompts the embarrassing question—if the Americans were all that religious, Christian, and Protestant, how come there is ''no mention of the Supreme Being, or of the Christian religion . . . in the Constitution?'' (118). Simple, Baird argued. It was not necessary because all the world knew that ''the Convention . . . was neither infidel nor atheistical in character. All the leading men in it were believers in Christianity, and Washington, as all the world knows, was a Christian'' (119). They formed a Constitution ''for a people already Christian'' whose acts ''gave ample evidence of their being favourable to religion'' (note how Baird simply equates ''religion'' with ''Christianity'' in the Thwackum tradition). Under the circumstances ''their doing nothing positive'' where religion was concerned, speaks ''more loudly than if they had expressed themselves in the most solemn formulas on the existence of the Deity and the truth of Christianity'' (104; note the adroit use of the argument, ''In the absence of proof to the contrary we may well assume that. . . .'').

Baird happily notes that the First Amendment means

that "the General Government shall not make any law for the support of any particular church, or of all the churches" (104). But he more happily notes that nothing "prohibits individual states from making such laws." And, more to his satisfaction if less accurate, he argues that nothing prohibits "the General Government . . . from promoting religion. . . ." (118), which, he claimed, was "the view of the subject taken by the proper authorities of the country" (118).

To Baird, standing squarely in the Thwackum tradition, "promoting religion" meant promoting Christianity only. With Mr. Justice Story whom he quoted, he could not conceive of " 'persons in this, or any other Christian country, who would deliberately contend that it was unreasonable or unjust to foster and encourage the Christian religion generally as a matter of sound policy, as well as of revealed truth' " (116). Here Baird had prestigious backing from eminent jurists in assuming that Christianity, being "part of the common law" (125) as in England, was "the law of the land" (119) and therefore "many offences still remain obnoxious to it, on the ground of their being contrary to the Christian religion."

On this basis Baird approved the 1811 indictment, trial, condemnation, fine, and imprisonment of the person in New York "for aspersing the character of Jesus Christ, and denying the legitimacy of his birth" (125). For, as he noted, Chief Justice Kent had argued that no government can " 'permit with impunity . . . the general religion of the community to be openly insulted and defamed . . .' " (125).

Baird, arguing at length that "the governments of the individual states [were] organized on the basis of

Christianity,'' generally approved the test oaths that were in their original Constitutions—especially that of South Carolina which required assent to a lengthy Protestant creed. By the same token he regretted that "the constitutions of the old states have since been deprived of what was exclusive in regard to religion, and [that] the political privileges of the Protestants are [now] extended to the Roman Catholics . . .'' (123–24).

It is specially to be noted that he used the word "privileges'' and not "rights.'' For to Baird, unlike Roger Williams and Thomas Jefferson, the rejection of formal Establishments was not a matter of principle and rights, but of convenience, expedience, and prudence. This would seem to be a direct denial of the intent of the First Amendment.

The absence of Established churches in the states, he argued, "is not . . . from any want of power . . . to create such an establishment, but because it has been found inexpedient to attempt promoting religion in that way'' (126). The men of the Constitutional Convention, he added "who loved it [Christianity] better than we do nowadays, felt bound in prudence to leave it at once unaided and unencumbered by constitutional provisions, save one or two of a negative character'' (119). Baird thus left the way open for the civil support of Christianity. For the implication of his argument is that what is deemed inexpedient and imprudent now, may not be judged so tomorrow. He was no defender of religious freedom in principle, and he mustered no theological arguments for it.[40]

To Baird religious liberty meant that only those "whose religious principles were not thought subversive of the great moral principles of Christianity were [to be] admitted to a full participation in civil privileges and immunities'' (124). So, while ''in every state the rights of conscience are guarantied [*sic*] to all men'' (124), we must not suppose this to mean ''that irreligion and licentiousness are also guarantied [*sic*] by the organic laws, or by any laws whatever.''

For ''rights of conscience are religious rights, that is, rights to entertain and utter religious opinions, and to enjoy public religious worship.'' But this ''cannot include irreligion; opinions contrary to the nature of religion, subversive of the reverence, love, and service due to God, of virtue, morality, and good manners.'' Indeed, he stormed, ''what rights of conscience can atheism, irreligion, or licentiousness pretend to?'' And while ''it may not be prudent to disturb them in their private haunts and secret retirements'' yet ''they have no right by any law in the United States . . . to propagate opinions and proselytize'' (125).[41]

But while this eminent graduate of Calvinistic Princeton could with the greatest of ease posthumously convert all the men who took part in the Constitutional Convention into sectarian Christians made over into his own image, he could not ignore what he called the ''very general impression'' prevalent in Europe, ''that the entire separation of Church and State in America was the work of Mr. Jefferson'' (106), and he somewhat grudgingly reprinted in a footnote ''the famous act 'for establishing religious freedom' drawn up by him . . .'' (110). Then he administers the *coup de grace* so often used by Christian controversialists—character assassination. ''None of Mr. Jefferson's admirers,'' he declared, ''will consider it slanderous to assert that he was a very bitter enemy to Christianity'' (106)—''one of the greatest enemies that Christianity has ever had to contend with in America'' (122)—and it is safe to ''assume that he wished to see not only the Episcopal Church separated from the State in Virginia, but the utter overthrow of everything in the shape of a church throughout the country'' (106). Indeed, Baird continues, Jefferson took pride in the ''famous act,'' but ''not because it embodied the principles of eternal justice, but because, by putting all religious sects on an equality, it seemed to degrade Christianity'' by comprehending, ''to use his [Jefferson's] own words, 'within the mantle of protection the Jew and the Gentile, the Christian and the Mohammedan, the Hindoo and infidel of every denomination' '' (111). ''It was this,'' Baird concluded, ''that made the arch-infidel chuckle with satisfaction—not, we repeat, that the great principles embodied in the measure were right'' (111).

Because the foundational principle of the Act is that ''Almighty God hath created the mind free, and manifested his supreme will that free it shall remain . . . ,'' it seems clear that Baird could not entertain the possibility that one not a Christian of his sectarian species could believe in God or creation.

It also seems clear enough that Baird's argument would undermine one's confidence in the premises and principles of the ''famous act'' as well as those of the Declaration and the Constitution. His younger contemporary, Horace Bushnell, was even more explicit.

Horace Bushnell (1802–1877), the prophet of nineteenth-century Protestantism's ''new theology'' (or ''progressive orthodoxy'') following *c.* 1850, became in the second quarter of the twentieth century the patron saint of religious educators who marched under Bushnell's slogan *''that the child is to grow up a Christian, and never know himself as being otherwise.''*[42] A many-dimensioned person with a homespun style (which he may have cultivated as did Robert Frost), he was a very eminent and influential preacher, original thinker, and prolific publisher of books.

In two sermons, the one in July 1861, the other in November 1864,[43] he essayed to make clear to his flock what the Civil War "means and the great moral and religious ideas that are struggling to the birth" in the "throes of adversity and sacrifice." In doing so he made perfectly clear his view of the relation between Christianity and government by the consent of the governed.

Holding that government is "legitimate and proper . . . only when it is a factor . . . in the Divine Government itself," Bushnell argued the impossibility of constructing a government "on mere grounds of philosophy . . . without some reference to a Supreme Being." He lamented, therefore, "the irreligious or . . . unreligious accident, by which our Constitution omits even the mention of God . . . ," and he approved efforts to have Him so recognized.[44] The omission, he argued, was not entirely accidental. For in the eighteenth century we Americans began "to conceive that we had certain inborn natural rights, and very soon also to maintain them by a stiff and sturdy assertion" which led to independence. But two lines of thought led to this conclusion and practical result.

On the one hand, some of "our leaders had been considerably affected by the political theories of Rousseau and other French infidel writers." These argued from "what they called nature and natural right in men" that "civil society . . . could only arise lawfully, by their consent, or compact, or vote" in which the people surrendered some "of their individual rights, to make up the public stock of powers and prerogatives in the state'' (PG, 293–94).

On the other hand, we Christians ''had been shaped historically by our popular training in the church, and the little democracies of our towns and colonial legislatures,'' and thus made as ''ready, as the others, to make a large assertion of our inborn, sacred rights and liberties'' (PG, 294).

Naturally ''the two schools flowed together, coalescing in the same declarations of right, and the same impeachments of wrong,'' and the same ''assertion of . . . independence.'' But under the pressures of time, we Christians accepted the ''famous July declaration'' without any ''nice consideration of our meaning, or precisely defined criticism of our principles,'' or ''very deliberate measurement of [its] ideas'' (PG, 294).

So ''New England and Virginia, Puritan church order and the doctrine of the French Encyclopedia'' were ''fused happily together in the language of Mr. Jefferson'' who was ''eminently crude'' enough duly to honor ''the 'Creator' and his friends'' by giving them ''a considerable place in a really atheistic bill or doctrine'' (PG, 294–95). Being an atheistic bill, the Declaration ''in the sense in which it is commonly understood . . . can only operate and has always operated destructively; working as a kind of latent poison against all government from the first day until now . . .'' (PG, 295).

Thus ''Mr. Jefferson . . . brought in modes of thought and philosophy . . . which are . . . bitterly pernicious'' and ''his name gained a currency for them that has made them even identical, as thousands really conceive, with our institutions themselves'' (RN, 169).

The Civil War, then, Bushnell argued, is the result of our trying to live on Jefferson's "nostrums of Atheistic philosophy" (PG, 311) and "trying to get up authority from below" while ignoring always "the fact [that] . . . 'there is no power but of God' " (PG, 310). Mr. Calhoun, building on Mr. Jefferson's "one miserably ambiguous and mischievously untrue maxim" that " 'sovereignty resides . . . in the people' " (PG, 306), concocted "what is called 'the State Rights doctrine' " (PG, 303), that brought on the Civil War. In brief, to Bushnell the Civil War was a contest between God and Jefferson.[45]

To Bushnell, that government is ordained of God as per Romans 13, meant that it descends from the top down.[46] So "we are born into civil society as we are into the atmosphere," and this "with as little right of consent as whether we should be born at all" (PG, 297). To be sure, magistrates "are in by election, but there is no passing over of powers in the vote." For "not one of the supposed powers was ever in the persons of the voters" but only in "the Constitution, the sanction of God's Head Magistracy going with it" (PG, 309). Herein Bushnell clearly denied the doctrine that sovereignty resides in the people.

Although the people "choose their magistrates" they do not govern them, but rather "the magistrates govern" the people. For "the magistrate is sovereign over the people, not they over him." The magistrate has "even a divine right to bind their conscience by his rule" (PG, 309).

Next Bushnell asserted that he knew "not where there is any such universal principle" as that "we are all, by nature, equally entitled to a government by consent.'' From his perspective, he said, ''A born magistracy, however unequal, be it kingly, or noble, is good without consent, if only it rule well'' (PG, 298). Indeed, ''our popular vote or choice is only one way of designating rulers, and the succession of blood another: both equally good and right when the historic order makes them so'' (RN, 173–74). To Bushnell as to Baird, democratic government is not a matter of rights and principle, but of expediency, prudence, and providence (history).

So Bushnell concluded that we would never have gotten into the Civil War if the whole idea of Christian rule ''had not been first loosened by the false maxims'' of government by the consent of the governed, and ''every bond of unity and dignity shivered by the pretentious usurpations of the state rights arguments and cabals'' derived from it. Now we are ''fighting out the most pestilent heresy of the nation''—''marching down these arguments pounding them down with artillery, never to stop marching, or stop pounding, till they are trampled so low and ground so fine that no search can find them'' (PG, 312–13).

So this gentle, kindly clergyman of staid Hartford, Connecticut, told his people that our cause against the ''mere human atheistic way of speaking . . . is especially God's'' (PG, 315), and we of the North ''catch heroic fire from God. Oh! it [this Civil War] is religion, it is God! Every drum-beat is a hymn, the cannon thunder God, the electric silence, darting victory along the wires, is the inaudible greeting of God's favoring word and purpose.'' Under God ''we are now in a way to have our free institutions crowned and consummated'' in the recognition of the truth of Romans 13: '' 'Let every soul be subject unto the higher powers; for there is no power but of God' '' (PG, 317).

In summary, Horace Bushnell's ecstatic vision of ''the great moral and religious'' meaning of the Civil War in which his people were engaged, was that the pernicious, ''mere human atheistic'' nostrums of Jefferson (among them apparently that ''Almighty God hath created the mind free'')—the doctrines of the sovereignty of the people, and government by consent of the governed—were being drowned in the ''Blood, blood, rivers of blood . . .'' of the fratricidal war that was ''especially God's.''

... when God has formed moral beings, even he can govern them ... only by moral influence and in accordance with the laws of mind.

LYMAN BEECHER, 1827

Almighty God hath created the mind free and manifested his supreme will that free it shall remain ...

THOMAS JEFFERSON, 1779

V

Enlightened Christianity and "The World's Last Hope"

I have suggested that during and following the eighteenth century the dominant species of Christianity in America was internalized and privatized, divorcing "salvation" from concern for the institutions of the convert's society; that meantime an authentic religious alternative to orthodox Christianity had emerged which I, following Crane Brinton, designate "Enlightenment"; that it was the theology of this new religion that provided legitimation for the institutional structures of the Republic, that a majority of the clerical leaders in defending their sectarian species of Christianity against the new religion tended to undermine their people's belief in the principles of the Republic; and that there are striking examples of eminent and powerful clergymen who bitterly opposed those principles—in the nineteenth century notably Robert Baird and Horace Bushnell.

As for general approach, I borrowed the concept of "case history" from Erik H. Erikson. A case history begins with the supposition that the subject is sick, and proceeds to probe his past for clues respecting the causes. The purpose is set by the supposition that once such causes are determined perhaps remedies can be devised and applied.

In more general form this is a common view of the purpose of all historical study, namely, to probe the past in such fashion as will enable us to understand the present situation in such a way as to guide us into the future. Abraham Lincoln stated it clearly in the "House Divided" speech in Springfield, Illinois, on June 16, 1858: "If we could first know where we are, and whither we are tending, we could better judge what to do, and how to do it."

I can see no serious use for the study of history except as a way of acquiring knowledge that is useful in the understanding and guidance of practical affairs. Like the house of the Father of Jesus, the discipline of history has many mansions, and my professional life is lived in the one called "American church history," or "American religious history," or, as I prefer because more exact, "religion in American history." This is an area long neglected by secular historians. But a decade ago Professor Henry F. May could rightly claim that "For the study and understanding of American culture, the recovery of American religious history may well be the most important achievement of the last thirty years. A vast and crucial area of American experience has [thereby] been rescued from neglect and misunder-standing." Assuming apparently the separation of the religious and intellectual lives in the United States, May suggested that the "literary intellectuals of the thirties" found that "theology was approachable partly because it seemed to have so little to do with religion, especially the religion of the First Methodist Church in the generic home town."[1] He might have said that the professors had rediscovered the clergy. Why and how they had lost sight of each other is a major theme in these essays.

At present there seems to be almost unanimous agreement among those in a position to know, that America's religious establishment is, as H. L. Mencken noted long ago, "down with a wasting disease."[2] If, as seems generally conceded, faith is the life blood of the movement, and the blood "is for the life thereof" as Leviticus (17:14) would have it, then the disease may fairly be described as a religious leukemia.

The conception of illness hangs upon a conception of what is "normal" for the organism in question. The conception of what *is* normal for it is based on such study of its past as enables one to form an opinion of the true nature of the organism and the functioning of its parts. Characteristic functioning is "normal," while uncharacteristic functioning and behavior is deemed "abnormal."

Christianity is almost 2,000 years old. Christendom, dated from the Council of Nicaea in 325, is almost 1,700 years old. The United States dated from the Declaration of Independence is only 200 years old. If we invoke as a standard for judging what is normal for the genus Christianity what seems to have been characteristic thinking and functioning in Christendom for fifteen centuries, some aspects of Christianity in the United States stand out in striking fashion as abnormal. I have suggested the following.

Assurance of salvation is internalized and institutionalized mediators made completely unnecessary or at
most, convenient but expendable, conveniences that
may aid the individual. There is religious pluralism
protected by the civil authority, which means that the
"secular" power protects the right of every citizen
openly to propagate any religious opinions he may
fancy, and actively to proselytize the members of other
groups so long as he does not overtly disturb the civil
peace. "Churches" have become voluntary associations, highly competitive not only among themselves
but with a complex congeries of other voluntary associations, all bidding for a share of the citizen's attention
and support. Theology, that is systematic and logically
coherent explanation and defense of the modes of
thought and action of a community of faith, has so
evaporated that even clergymen often hold at least two
mutually exclusive theologies at the same time.[3] It is
widely supposed and often vehemently argued that
religion has nothing to do with the social, political,
and economic orders of the society. And, finally, at
important points the basic principles and premises of
the dominant religious establishment are at war with
the fundamental principles and premises of the civil
order in which the church-member-citizen lives.

Whatever one may think of these characteristics of
our contemporary religious scene, and however one may
evaluate them—whether, for example, as evidences of
"progress" or of degradation and decadence—they *are*
abnormalities if what prevailed during fifteen centuries
of Christendom is invoked as the standard for judging
what is normal functioning and behavior for this genus
of religion.

Among these symptoms of religious leukemia it has seemed to me that the unresolved tensions between the premises of the dominant religious establishment of the nation and those of the civil order are of primary importance. This view, which is inherent and sometimes explicit in all my work, is now widely recognized and accepted. It seems implicit, for example, in the analysis of sociologists Parsons and Shils that a society is bound to be sick when its "cultural system" is at odds with its "social system." Or, using the concepts and language of anthropologist Ruth Benedict, when the norms commonly professed in a community are contradicted by the norms implicit in generally accepted practice, the society is at least on the way to becoming schizophrenic.[4]

In Chapter IV I illustrated in the works of Robert Baird and Horace Bushnell strikingly clear examples of overt rejection of the premises of the Declaration and Constitution on the basis of what they held to be not only normal, but normative Christianity. Bushnell, especially, clearly offered his people a choice between his species of Christianity and the fundamental principles of the Republic in which they lived. To him the Civil War was a contest between "Christ" and "Jefferson" in which the latter's "atheistic nostrums" were happily being drowned in the "blood, blood, rivers of blood" of the fratricidal struggle.

Baird and Bushnell, although more outspoken than most, are, I think, typical of a dominant strand in the species of Christianity most prevalent in the United States.

There was another strand, now largely forgotten, in which the principles and premises of the Republic were legitimated by a theology "distinctively Christian" even according to Professor Hudson's standard. It is to be seen in the work of Lyman Beecher (1775–1863), a very eminent and powerful leader of New England's Congregational orthodoxy during the first half of the nineteenth century—now commonly known, if at all, only as the father of Henry Ward Beecher and Harriet Beecher Stowe. If you wish to live in history beware of having famous children.

But before I take up Beecher's model of the relation between Christianity and the Republic it behooves me to delineate the theoretical framework that makes my evaluation understandable. Unfortunately, both this and treatment of Beecher's perspective involve the use of a certain amount of technical jargon. There are areas in the life of the Western religious mind that cannot be made simple. Having observed the success of the theology of *Peanuts,* if I could do it over again I would be tempted to delve professionally only in an area of knowledge that can be adequately conveyed in cartoons.

While not presuming to be an intellectual historian in the technical sense, I agree with John C. Greene that "the primary function of the intellectual historian is to delineate the presuppositions of thought in given historical epochs . . . to search for and describe those most general ideas, or patterns of ideas, which inform the thought of the age."[5] That, I think, states my primary purpose.

Whether intended or not, Greene's view of intellectual history fits neatly into the context provided by philosopher A. N. Whitehead, from whose *Adventures of Ideas* I cheerfully admit that I cribbed most of my philosophy of history. Whitehead postulates that ''in each period [of history] there is a general form of the forms of thought'' that is ''so pervading . . . that only by extreme effort can we become aware of it.'' These ideas of highest generality that characterize an era ''rarely receive any accurate verbal expression'' but are hinted at in forms of art, literature, poetry, rituals, etc. They are implicit, that is assumed, in the rational discourse of a period, which moves on the level of ''derivative specialized notions of violent controversy. The intellectual strife of an age is mainly concerned with these latter questions of secondary generality which conceal a general agreement upon first principles almost too obvious to need expression, and almost too general to be capable of expression.''[6]

So Whitehead, Greene and I would advise that if you want to understand a period, including our own, do not give chief ''attention to those intellectual positions which its exponents feel it necessary explicitly to defend,'' but look for ''some fundamental assumptions which adherents of all the variant systems within the epoch unconsciously presuppose.''[7] To delineate them is most difficult and a rare achievement for, as Whitehead put it, ''It requires a very unusual mind to undertake the analysis of the obvious.''[8]

Granted this theoretical framework, as historians we are bound, knowingly or not, to evaluate the mental calibre of the thinkers of an era on the basis of the extent to which they seem to have sensed ''the form of the forms of thought'' of their time and built their explanation and defense of their species of religion and/or their social, political and economic theories on that foundation. For only insofar can they be said to have been "with it" in their generation.

My thesis is that Isaac Backus, who, as McLoughlin argues, is representative of nineteenth-century evangelicals in general, and Robert Baird and Horace Bushnell specifically, either were not "with it" in this sense, or if, as did Baird and Bushnell, they seemed to sense the basic "form of the forms of thought" of their time, they feared its implications and retreated to the anachronistic theologies of the pre-Revolutionary period. We, being aware as Muller reminds us, that "the self-evident truths rehearsed in the Declaration of Independence had not been at all evident to the leaders of Christendom for some seventeen centuries,"[9] can understand why they failed to recognize the master ideal of their time and place, put their faith in the supposed security of the traditional perspective of Christendom, and tried to force the new experience in the New World into the old theological wineskins developed during the supposed golden age of Christianity. They are ideal types of reaction against basic principles of the Republic in the name of their peculiar species of the Establishment religion of their land.

Lyman Beecher represents a counter type. In contrast to his younger contemporaries, he was as much "with it" in his time as was Thomas Jefferson. This means, in the context sketched above, that Beecher and Jefferson began with and built upon the same high general idea—the master ideal—of their era. And they used practically identical words in pointing to it.

God, said Jefferson in private, "has formed us moral agents."[10] "Almighty God hath created the mind free, and manifested his supreme will that free it shall remain,''[11] he declared in formal public statement.

In the beginning, said Beecher, "God . . . formed moral beings, [and] even he can govern them, as such, only by moral influence, and in accordance with the laws of mind," for "mere omnipotence [is] . . . as irrelevant to the government of mind as moral influence would be to the government of the physical world."[12]

Beecher was distinctively, even awesomely "Christian." With his friend and alter-ego, Nathaniel William Taylor, professor of theology at Yale Divinity School from 1822 to 1858, he led the defense of Connecticut's species of orthodoxy against the "infidels" and then against the Boston Unitarians. In passing through Yale College during the second half of the 1790s under the tutelage of Timothy Dwight, Beecher was programmed to defend Connecticut's style of civil support for the public worship of God. But, in his terms, God by permitting the "Toleration" party to win in 1818 and bring about disestablishment, taught him that such Establishment was contrary to belief in free moral agency and destructive of civil and religious liberty. It was a hard lesson. Looking back on it Beecher confessed that he "suffered what no tongue can tell" before he realized that disestablishment was *"the best thing that ever happened to the State of Connecticut."*[13]

Certainly it was the best thing that ever happened to Lyman Beecher. For this providential lesson unified his thinking and acting and induced him to work out the theological and practical implications of free agency for civil and ecclesiastical life in the Republic in a way that even Jefferson could have approved. The result has made him a puzzle both to many of his contemporaries and to following generations of historians, because he does not fit neatly into any of the commonly used interpretative categories.

It might be said, for example, that in theology he was an orthodox, Connecticut, Congregational, Yale "Calvinist" (a unique species), while in politics he was definitely of the "Jeffersonian" stripe. Although he was himself a mighty revivalist, and the teacher and leader of revivalists, he had no patience with the central thrust of the revival tide which, as we have noted, was to separate "salvation" from responsibility for and involvement in the societal life of the commonwealth. These differences placed him on the periphery of the main currents of nineteenth-century evangelical life represented politically, for example, by Baird and Bushnell. Because in his model of the relation between the premises of traditional evangelical orthodoxy and those of modern democracy he blazed one path to their reconciliation, it deserves more extensive and careful analysis than it has received or I can give in this essay.[14]

I suppose that in whatever words expressed, every system begins with conceptions of God, nature, and man. For these are the foci of the complex conception of "the nature of things." Lyman Beecher began with God's creation of moral beings who can be governed as such only by moral influence. The implication of this position, devastating for much of Christian orthodoxy, was stated by his son Charles: "By moral government we mean a system where the divine agency is related to, and limited by, the freedom of the creature will."[15] This, to anticipate, made Christianity "*a principle of action."* Converts entered the church militant, the company of saints "conflicting with their enemies upon earth" as the authors of the Cambridge Platform of 1648 had put it.[16] Because he held that "the divine agency is . . . limited by, the freedom of the creature will" to Beecher the conflict was real, the enemy tangible and powerful.

The Bible, God's revelation, Beecher argued, was a code of "the laws of a moral government."[17] A moral government operates through "the influence of law upon accountable creatures" (SVO 139). Law "includes precepts" disclosing "what is to be done," and sanctions presenting "the motives to obedience in . . . terms of reward and punishment." So "the influence of law . . . is the influence of motives upon accountable creatures; and the effect . . . is always the actual exercise of free agency; in choice or action" (SVO 140). Law therefore, does not "destroy free agency; for it is the influence of persuasion only" on accountable creatures who have "understanding, to perceive the rule of action; conscience, to feel moral obligations; and the faculty of choice in the view of motives" (SVO 139). Beecher recognized that free agency can operate only "by the exhibition of motives to voluntary agents." Hence he held that God's moral government of man-kind "is the influence of law upon the affections and conduct of intelligent accountable creatures" (SVO 141–42).

Hence he argued that the Bible as a code of laws, reveals a "system of precepts and motives" which has two parts. "There is the moral law in ten command-ments, and its summary import comprised in [the] two" great commandments. This moral law provides "a rule of life'' for all men. But there is also the Gospel, ''composed, no less than the [moral] law, of precepts enforced by sanctions.'' The Gospel assumes and ''adopts the moral law.'' But ''as a system of salvation, it [adds and prescribes] its own specific duties of repentance and faith, enforced by its own . . . sanctions'' (SVO 142–43).

Beecher noted that certain doctrines are essential to the moral law as a rule of life for all men, and mentioned ''The being of God; the accountability of man; a future state of reward and punishment without end; and a particular providence taking cognizance of human conduct in reference to future retribution'' (SVO 158–59). These will readily be recognized as the typical deist's ''essentials of every religion,'' as Franklin called them. So when Beecher asked, ''Are not these fundamental?'' he could be sure that all enlightened intellectuals, whether orthodox or deist, would answer ''yes.''

On this basis Beecher was in complete agreement with the ''enlightened'' thinkers of the day so far as civil government and the choice of civil rulers was concerned. Christians, he argued, are not bound to confine or regulate their ''suffrages . . . exclusively with reference to [the] piety or doctrinal opinions'' of the candidates. They need only look for ''such a belief in the being of God, and of accountability and future punishment, as lays a foundation for the practical influence of an oath,'' such moral conduct as will set a good example; ''general approbation of the christian religion and its institutions, as will dispose them to afford to religion the proper protection and influence of government.''

But this did not mean to Beecher official government

support of his species of Christianity. Rather, the candidate must exhibit only such "exemption from sectarian zeal" as will assure "the confidence of other denominations"; and his "administration [must be] impartial in its aspect upon all of them."

Granted these generally desirable characteristics, and Christians may "repose confidence in men, for civil purposes, who do not [even] profess religion, or afford evidence of piety." To suppose that as Christians they are forbidden to do so is to make the disastrous "mistake of our pious [New England] fathers" who made "the terms of communion and civil trust the same," thus obliterating the line between church and world and destroying the channels through which God's moral government is brought to mankind (SVO-247–48).

Two things are notable here. Beecher flatly rejected the theocratic ideal of his Puritan ancestors, and insofar ceased to be a Calvinist in the traditional sense; and he clearly enunciated the principle of civil neutrality toward the sectarian claims of the religious groups which has played such a large part in Supreme Court decisions on matters pertaining to religion. He, unlike Baird and Bushnell, elaborated an orthodox Christian legitimation of the basic principles of the Republic— that sovereignty resides in "the people," and that government must be by the consent of the governed.

He remained orthodox in his conception of salvation and an ardent defender of "The Faith Once Delivered to the Saints" (SVO 217–96). Man, he held, is not saved through obedience to the moral law alone. For he "is a sinner,—his heart is unholy,—and new affections are demanded"—a change of heart that is effected only by the Gospel, the "system of salvation."

The Gospel is "a system of moral influence, for the restoration of man from sin to holiness" (SVO 159), and as such it "prescribes its own specific duties of repentance and faith" which have their "own most glorious and fearful sanctions" (SVO 143). There is, for example, "the exhibition of [the] danger" of damnation to induce the necessary fear; the "disclosure of guilt" in the sight of God to motivate repentance; inculcation of a sense of unworthiness to induce humility; implanting a sense "of guilt and helplessness" to induce the sense of complete dependence; and, finally, the creation of confidence in the "divine sufficiency [of] . . . the Saviour" to induce faith (SVO 159).

These steps will be recognized as the stock-in-trade of practically all evangelical revivalists—the stages through which the preacher must lead the prospective convert to his species of Christianity. Beecher held that the proper preaching of the fundamental doctrines of Christianity, for example, the Trinity, total depravity, justification by faith, eternal punishment or felicity, etc., was the only effective instrument.

But most striking from a defender of New England orthodoxy in 1817 is Beecher's assertion that there is "no specific and formal command" that these doctrines "shall be believed" for salvation. For, he argued, "these come under the head of motives; and who ever heard of a special enactment requiring subjects to believe the declarations of a lawgiver, with respect to the motives of obedience?" (SVO 169). It is implied that any other motives if efficacious in inducing repentance and faith would be equally acceptable, for apparently the traditional doctrinal forms are merely means to that desired end.

Formally Beecher defined man's duty very much as had James Madison and the deists. It is to obey the will of his Creator. This means, Beecher argued, that "If men, as accountable creatures, are bound to act as God commands, they are bound to understand those doctrines which disclose the principles and motives of action . . ." (SVO 169). And if they are to understand them they must be stated in language they can understand. It follows, he held, that any "proposition which is the precise object of faith, is never unintelligible, but is always definite and plain" (SVO 154). In brief, for salvation man is not required to believe any unintelligible propositions.[18]

The infidel differs from the Christian in supposing that "the light of nature is man's only guide" (SVO 152). Beecher granted that the character of God is disclosed "by his work and by his word" (SVO 138), that is, in the creation as well as in the Bible, and he quoted one of the few Biblical texts that made sense to Thomas Paine, " 'The heavens declare his glory, and the firmament showeth his handy work' " (SVO 138). Beecher even conceded that "these disclosures of the heavens" were sufficient to "create obligation and discover guilt," but argued that this was "not sufficient to restrain the depravity of man, nor to disclose an atonement for him, nor to announce terms of pardon, nor to sanctify the soul" (SVO 138). This is disclosed only in the Bible, the other volume of God's single revelation.[19]

Both the volume of nature, and the Bible must be interpreted by reason. But salvation is discovered only in the second, which demands obedience to the Scriptures *both* as "a rule of life" for all men, *and* as "a system of salvation." This requires understanding of the truths, observation of the duties of the moral law, and the "repentance and faith required by the Gospel" (SVO 143).

Beecher was no antinomian. There must be, he asserted, a "coincidence of holiness in the Heart with overt deeds . . . to constitute [saving] obedience" (SVO 162). These are the requirements therefore for membership in a visible church of Christ. This means that the Christian must assume responsibility for *all* the institutions of his society as an aspect of, and overt evidence of, saving faith.

Here Beecher confronted the primordial "puritan dilemma" so ably spelled out by Edmund Morgan—how can Christians and their churches manage to live and exert their commanded influence in the affairs of the world without becoming worldly?[20]

Beecher was quite orthodox in supposing that there were "but two classes of men." All men are either holy or unholy. There can be "no middle ground" (SVO 189), for where obedience is commanded "neutrality would be disobedience."[21] Every Christian "is bound to confess Christ before men, and to enrol [*sic*] himself as a member of some visible church" (SVO 196). The qualifications for membership are *"personal holiness in the sight of God, and a credible profession of holiness before men"* (SVO 188). On becoming a member one assumes the awful responsibility of passing judgment on the genuineness of the holiness of prospective members, bolstered by the assumption that "the commands of God are the measure . . . of human ability" (SVO 76).

A church made up of such members and constituted by a compact, is *"a society incorporated by the God of*

heaven with specific chartered privileges" (SVO 184).
Among the rights of its members are "the election of
their own officers, . . . the framing of their own
articles of faith, and the ordering of their own worship
and discipline, according to their conception of the
word of God" (SVO 184). In this Beecher was closely
following the authors of the Cambridge Platform of
1648 as seen through the eyes of a nineteenth-century
evangelical Christian.

But Beecher went beyond both in asserting that "the
organization [of a true church] is such as may embody,
and ultimately will embody, the population of the
world" (SVO 184), that is, a local church exercising its
God-given rights is the model for all civil as well as
ecclesiastical government. Civil and religious freedom
are but obverse sides of the same providential march
toward the millennium. The gathered churches are the
leaven in the monstrous lump of the moral universe.

For churches so conceived and so dedicated are "the
organized administrators of the influence of the divine
moral government" (SVO 363) on earth, and as such
they are the link between Gospel and law, the "system
of salvation" and the "rule of life," the divine moral
government and human governments. They are the
repositories of true religion, the "master spring" of all
"our laws, habits, and manners." If it is removed
"every movement will stop . . . the soul depart, . . . the
body die" (SVO 128).

There is more than a hint in Beecher that the struggle
is real and that God may not win. He asserted that "if
the purposes of sin go into operation, the purposes of
God are defeated. If sin succeeds, the kingdom of God
fails" (SVO 18). He had assurance only that "the great
plan of government which God has chosen, and which

his power and wisdom will execute, will embrace as much good as is in the nature of things possible" (SVO 15).

Always, he argued, "the cause of God on earth has been maintained and carried forward only by . . . heroic exertion" and "propagated . . . by stupendous efforts" (SVO 280). The word of Command, he said, is not "Stand, but MARCH" (SVO 280), and Christians cannot sit back, "trust Providence, and expect that God will vindicate His cause while we neglect the use of appropriate means." We must make "such exertions . . . as the exigency demands and we are able to make."[22] He had no use for quietism. Unlike many of his evangelical contemporaries, he could not separate "salvation" from social and political responsibility. His view was that "among real Christians religion is a predominant principle of action."[23]

No doubt Beecher was intrigued by the wonderful world of Newton—the image of a universe held together only by the perfect balance between motion and gravity that maintained the harmony of the spheres. In the moral universe depravity was analogous to motion—the centrifugal force—and the Gospel was analogous to gravity—the centripetal force. The moral world exists in the heart of mankind. And because man by creation is a free agent, these two forces contending within him are matters of choice. So when God proclaimed "I have set before you life and death, . . . therefore choose life" (Deut. 30:19), the choice was real. Beecher concluded that Christians, united in "regularly organized churches," are called to use available means, indeed, to do "whatever may be necessary" (SVO 140) to maintain the nice balance between depravity and Gospel. For, Beecher argued, in the moral universe "nothing but [such] an impulse carefully and constantly applied, will keep things in their proper course" (SVO 137). And "the Lord Jesus Christ has decided, that regularly organized churches" must provide that impulse (SVO 363).

This view provides a theological context for the concept of the nice moral balance necessary for the institutions of free men that was stated by James Madison in the fifty-fifth Federalist Paper: "As there is a degree of depravity in mankind which requires a certain degree of circumspection and distrust, so there are other qualities in human nature which justify a certain portion of esteem and confidence." Our generation probably knows the sentiment best in Reinhold Niebuhr's apt paraphrase: "Man's capacity for justice makes democracy possible; but man's inclination to injustice makes democracy necessary."[24]

We have noted that Beecher placed Providence among the essential beliefs as did the deists. Belief in Providence was not a specialized notion, nor a propositional truth subject to the judgment of true or false. It was a presupposition which Franklin, as a typical deist, placed among the things he "never doubted." It was an assertion of the obvious—a feeling that purpose pervaded the universe and every discrete event found its meaning only in relation to that purpose. Lincoln expressed it as confidence that "we cannot but believe that he who made the world still governs it."[25]

In such a world the will of God prevails and freedom consists in acting according to His will. Providence means that the question asked of every experience, and especially of adverse experiences, is, what is God trying to teach me—what am I to learn from it? Assuming that God controls everything that happens, it follows that He communicates to me what He wants me to do next through "the signs of the times," that is, through the experienced events of the history-that-happens.[26]

History, in the context of belief in Providence as Beecher always saw it, is studied for clues to from whence we came, where we are, and whither tending as a basis for judging what to do and how to do it. From his knowledge of history Beecher concluded that he lived in a revolutionary epoch, and that eventually all governments "will, under some form, become so far popular in their spirit, as that political power shall be in the hands of the people" (SVO 297). Thus Beecher, unlike Baird and Bushnell, asserted his belief in what Tocqueville called the dogma of the sovereignty of the people.

With the establishment, or re-establishment, of true churches following the Reformation, he argued, an example of such government was given to the world, and, "all . . . indications, seem to declare the purpose of God to employ this nation in the glorious work . . ." (SVO 303) of furthering the spread of civil and religious liberty. Indeed, "this nation has been raised up by providence to exert an efficient instrumentality in this work of moral renovation" (SVO 295).

How is this work to be done? The divine influence administered by the churches is incarnated in the civil institutions of democracy, which in turn create a society favorable to the being and continuation of such churches. Prosperity in the churches has always "been aided by the civil condition of the world," Beecher noted, and the "rapid and universal extension of civil and religious liberty" in the world today is "introductory to the triumphs of universal Christianity" in the millennium.[27] So conceived, the millennium is to be *in* history, and movement toward it *is* history.

But before the millennium can arrive, Beecher argued, "great changes are required in the civil and religious condition of nations" (SVO 295). First, "the monopoly of the soil . . . by kings, and military chieftains, and nobles . . . must be abolished" and the earth returned to "those who till it." For "the possession of the earth . . . by the cultivator, is the great principle of action in the moral world" (SVO 295–96). Second, "the monopoly of power must be superseded by the suffrages of freemen," for as long as "the great body of the people are excluded from all voice and influence in legislation, it is impossible" to create a society "such as the faculties of man allow, and the word of God predicts" (SVO 296). Third, "the rights of conscience must . . . be restored to man." This means that "governments and ecclesiastics . . . must cease to dictate what men shall believe, and in what manner they shall worship God" (SVO 297). It is not difficult to recognize here the elements of Jefferson's program to destroy the old aristocracies.[28]

We are not to suppose, Beecher continued, that these changes being brought about by "the progress of truth will be without resistance" (SVO 291). It is naive to think that the monopolizers of the land, the usurpers of power, and the dictators of belief will relinquish "spontaneously" what they have stolen from the people. It must be wrested from them. To bring about "these changes in the civil and religious condition of the world, revolutions and convulsions are doubtless indispensable" (SVO 298). And "revolutions . . . are predicted" that shall "shake the earth with violence of nation dashing against nation;—until every despotic government shall be thrown down." But over the resulting chaos "the spirit of God shall move again . . . and bring out a new creation" (SVO 298).[29]

The revolutionary power resides in the common people. In his *Lectures on Political Atheism* Beecher confessed that he had learned that "the heart and bones and sinews of liberty are with the labouring men of my country—the agriculturists, artisans, and all sorts of labourers. And I know that, unperverted, they will defend her institutions forever." You, he said to laborers, are the "best and last hope of my country," and "I hope to be admitted into your fraternity. . . . For, besides my own direct claims, all my American ancestors were farmers or artisans."[30]

The flood tide of revolution is rising in the common people throughout the world, and is sweeping all the old tyrannies before it as it flows toward the millennium sea of universal political and religious freedom. And, in Beecher's view, that flood was created, and could continue to be fed only by innumerable little freshets of divine impulse trickling out of the many pure churches scattered over the land. Such was his vision of the nature and purpose of true churches, and of the destiny of the Republic, "this most blessed experiment, the world's last hope" (SVO 359).

Beecher, born in October 1775, grew up in the atmosphere of the ideological revolution that culminated during the last quarter of the eighteenth century.[31]

That revolution brought all absolute rulers, even God, under the rule of law.[32] The movement is reflected in the many treatises produced by New England divines during that period to explain and defend "the justice of God in the damnation of sinners." Merely to say with Saint Paul that the omnipotent potter has "power over the clay: of the same lump to make one vessel unto honour, and another unto dishonour" (Romans 9:21) no longer played even in pious New England. Beecher clearly saw that mankind has choice of just two forms of government—by men or by law—that the people must either submit knowingly and willingly to laws in the making of which they participate, or unwillingly to the coercion of a tyrant (SVO 92).[33]

And, he argued, that the only government consistent with free agency is government by the consent of the governed—"a free government . . . a government of laws made by the people" (SVO 40). Here Beecher differed radically from his younger contemporaries, Robert Baird and Horace Bushnell. For Beecher such free government was a matter of principle rooted in the created nature of man. For them it was merely a matter of prudence and expedience. Baird implied and Bushnell clearly declared that monarchy, aristocracy, or any other form was in principle equally good. This is to say that unlike Beecher's model, their professed theology did not legitimate the structure of the government under which they lived—that their cultural system was at war with their social system—that they divorced "salvation" from responsible involvement in the society in which they lived.

Beecher was realistic in recognizing that in a free government the real ruler is "the opinion of the

people'' or ''public opinion'' (SVO 50). It follows that
''laws in republics depend for their prompt execution
upon a correct and efficient public sentiment'' (SVO
45). For no law can be enforced if public opinion is
against it (SVO 195).[34]

He also saw that such ''public sentiment'' in a
people does not just happen. It results from the
reasoned exertion of ''moral influence'' (SVO 92) on
the ''spring of action,'' their motives (SVO 195). Only
''the moral influence of religious institutions'' can
make ''civil laws'' effectively prevail. The two are but
the obverse sides of government. As ''civil law cannot
reach the spring of action,'' neither can ''religion, by
her moral influence alone . . . arrest the arm of
violence or punish the encroachments upon life and
society'' (SVO 195). This means that ''in a free
government moral suasion and coercion must be
united''—''the influence of education and habit''
must be backed by civil authority or ''restraints will
be swept away by the overpowering force of human
depravity'' (SVO 85).

Because the people are sovereign ''the mass'' must
be imbued ''with knowledge and virtue'' if the Republic is to live.[35] For ''unless the salt of the earth
contained in Christian institutions can be diffused
through the land, the mass will putrify'' (SVO 311). It
is through education that the churches apply their moral
influence and exert their revolutionary power. And,
Beecher reminded his hearers, ''neither talent nor
piety will supersede the necessity for application . . .
you must act'' (SVO 130).[36]

But the churches must act in the commonwealth
without jeopardizing their purity by assuming civil
authority in Establishments, and/or taking sides on
specific issues and thus becoming embroiled in im-

mediate political and social problems. And they can do this, Beecher insisted, by creating voluntary associations or "Societies" which are the "providential substitutes" for the old legal supports given by Establishments (SVO 311).

Such a Society is not a church, and not an arm of the churches made up of church members only.[37] It is a voluntary association, the sole purpose of which is to create or bolster a proper public sentiment on one given issue. To get anything done in a republic, Beecher realized, there must be "concert of action," and the purpose of a Society is to create such concert (SVO 58). He recognized that in a pluralistic commonwealth of free agents things get done only through a more or less temporary alliance or coalition of very diverse persons, each of whom happens to be interested in furthering a specific cause, each for his own reasons.

The genius of a Society is that, concentrating on one specific objective, it can enlist the support of all kinds and conditions of men regardless of their piety or lack of it, or their personal reasons for giving their support. Unlike a church, a Society need not inquire into the motives of a prospective supporter, and if it does so it severely limits the number of those who will contribute to it. It is based on the principle of the plurality of principles, as is the Republic itself.[38]

Beecher saw all this clearly as early as 1811 when, in promoting the Connecticut Bible Society he exulted that "Churchmen [i.e., Episcopalians] and Democrats, Christians and men of the world, all fall into the ranks . . . The thing is the most popular of any public charity ever attempted in Connecticut."[39]

Societies so conceived constituted Beecher's practical answer to the question of how the churches can remain holy and unworldly while doing their job as "the

organized administrators of the influence of the divine
moral government'' in the world. The moral impulse,
that is, the impetus behind all movement toward the
ideal millennium in all the institutions of society was
channeled by God through true churches. It was assumed that all important social issues are moral questions, and therefore the business of the churches. It
was also assumed that until the millennium was
ushered in, good and evil exist side by side in this
world, all with God's permission.[40] Because he assumed
this, Beecher saw clearly that it was not enough to be
against evil in general. The churches to be effective in
exercising their moral responsibility for the world, had
to provide the impetus to attack specific problems one
by one, without actually becoming involved in the
immediate worldly issues. Societies, each aimed against
one specific evil or the promotion of one specific good,
were the providential means provided. While the moral
incentive originated in the churches, such voluntary
associations were independent of the churches and were
not the churches in action, they did provide ''an
influence . . . distinct from that of the government,
independent of popular suffrage, superior in potency to
individual efforts, and competent to enlist and preserve
the public opinion . . .'' (SVO 86) on the side of
right.[41]

In summary, Lyman Beecher, born in 1775, was
religiously immersed in Connecticut's peculiar species
of Puritan orthodoxy, and matured in the political
atmosphere of the revolutionary thinking that lay
behind the War for Independence and the launching of
the first new nation. These two strands in his makeup
were bound together by his inherited sense of Providence, which meant that everything experienced happened by God's permission. From this perspective it

was impossible either to ignore any development or rigidly to adhere to the particular forms of any orthodoxy. The first question to be asked of every experience was, What is God trying to teach us by permitting this to happen?

This made his biblically based evangelical theological system as open-minded as that of "Enlightenment." Beecher remained all his life a passionate supporter of both the Protestant evangelical orthodoxy that lay behind the denominations' revivalistic and missionary thrust of the nineteenth century, and the principles of the new democratic-republican government which many fellow evangelicals, here represented by Baird and Bushnell, rejected. His work is significant because he bridged the gap between them (as William Ellery Channing bridged the gap between eighteenth-century "Enlightenment" and nineteenth-century romanticism in its American transcendentalist dress).

Such bridge figures always perplex and usually irritate those who tend to see the whole truth on one side of an issue in a situation where the two sides have been polarized as Beecher's mentor, Timothy Dwight, had worked to polarize Christianity and "infidelity." Beecher, an activist of high visibility because involved in most and prominent in several of the ecclesiastical and political movements of his time, was naturally suspect by those of both sides. This explains why he has often been written off by "either/or"-minded critics as adhering consistently to no basic principles but operating purely on grounds of immediate expediency and a timid prudence—as being on both sides of every issue, specifically for example, of being both a colonizationist and an abolitionist.

Actually his was a surprisingly complete, consistent, and coherent system of biblical theology that made sense out of what was going on about him and explained within that context his many diverse activities and shifts in position. His was, I think, a striking example of what Cushing Strout has dubbed a "political religion," that is, he was one who made "a politics out of religion" as contrasted with those who make "a religion out of politics."[42] In extreme form the difference is between those who worship God and those who worship the particular forms of a church or a state—a confusion of ends and means.

Lyman Beecher represented a way that might have enabled Christianity to avoid such pitfalls into which it has stumbled in America, i.e., the separation of "salvation" from social and political responsibility; the appearance of offering a choice between being a faithful church member and being an informed and loyal citizen of the Republic, with consequent bifurcation of the minds of many church members; the erosion of the denominations' theology because irrelevant to the life of the commonwealth; the separation and discrete institutionalization of the nation's religious and intellectual lives; and the death of the theologian as significant intellectual in the society.

I load myself with these borrowings more and more heavily every day beyond my intention and my original form, following the fancy of the age and the exhortation of others. If it is unbecoming to me, as I believe it is, no matter; it may be useful to someone else.

MONTAIGNE, "Of Physiognomy"

I, among so many borrowings of mine, am very glad to be able to hide one now and then, disguising and altering it for a new service. At the risk of letting it be said that I do so through failure to understand its original use, I give it some particular application with my own hand, so that it may be less purely someone else's.

Ibid.

Notes

INTRODUCTION

1. R. G. Collingwood, *An Essay on Metaphysics* (Oxford: Clarendon Press, 1940), p. 198.

2. Edward W. Cronin, Jr., "The Yeti," in *Atlantic Monthly*, 236, 5 (November, 1975), 50.

3. *The Complete Essays of Montaigne*, trans. by Donald M. Frame (Stanford University Press, 1965), p. 786.

4. Alfred North Whitehead, *Adventures of Ideas* (New York: The Free Press, 1967), p. 163.

5. *Ibid.*, pp. 166-67. The argument here is built on insights from the whole of chapter ten of this book, "The New Reformation," pp. 160-72.

6. *Ibid.*, p. 12.

7. *Ibid.*, pp. 168-69.

8. *Ibid.*, pp. 168-69.

9. *Ibid.*, p. 18.

10. Harvey Cox, *The Seduction of the Spirit* (New York: Simon and Schuster, 1973), p. 17.

11. Ralph Waldo Emerson, "An Address" (commonly known as "The Divinity School Address"), in Brooks Atkinson, ed., *The Complete Essays and Other Writings of Ralph Waldo Emerson* (New York: The Modern Library, 1940), pp. 83-84.

12. *Adventures of Ideas,* p. 18.

13. For more extensive definitions and implications, see Chapter III of my *The Nation with the Soul of a Church* (New York: Harper & Row, 1975), pp. 29-47.

CHAPTER I

1. Ralph Waldo Emerson, "Experience," in Brooks Atkinson, ed., *The Selected Writings of Ralph Waldo Emerson* (New York: Modern Library, 1950), p. 342.

2. Alfred North Whitehead, *Adventures of Ideas* (New York: Free Press, 1967), p. 47.

3. Thornton Wilder, *The Eighth Day* (New York: Popular Library, 1967), p. 347.

4. Edmund Spenser in *The Faerie Queene* (Canto vi, Stanzas 29-39) delineates a form of the myth of eternal creation out of the chaos in the imagery of the garden of Adonis wherein occurs the perpetual incarnation of life in forms the matter for which comes out of the "huge eternal Chaos." J. C. Smith and E. DeSelincourt, eds., *Spenser Poetical Works* (London: Oxford University Press, 1966), pp. 174-75.

5. *Macbeth,* Act III, Scene 1.

6. Walter Kerr, *The Decline of Pleasure* (New York: Time, Inc., 1966), p. 146.

7. Robert Kellogg and Oliver Steele, eds., *Edmund Spenser, Books I and II of the Faerie Queene, The Mutability Cantos, and Selections from the Minor Poetry* (Indianapolis: The Odyssey Press, 1965), pp. 399, 409, 435-36.

8. Edmund Spenser, *The Faerie Queene,* Book III, Canto vi, stanza 47, in Smith and DeSelincourt, eds., *Spenser Poetical Works,* p. 176.

In this view, couched in the imagery of the garden of Adonis, life itself is immortal although it appears in innumerable particular forms all of which are subject to mortality (Mutability). A sophisticated contemporary version of this perspective is found in the works of Loren Eiseley, and made very clear in his book, *The Immense Journey* (of life on this planet).

9. Hebrews 11:1, Jerusalem Bible version.

10. For what I mean by *sectarian* see Chapter III of my *The Nation With the Soul of a Church* (New York: Harper & Row, 1975), pp. 29-47.

11. Hamlet, Act III, Scene 2.

12. Eiseley refers to the time when "Man . . . 'crossed over' into this new invisible environment" which exists only "in man's brain, in his way of looking at the World around him and at the social environment he was beginning to create in his tiny human groupings." *The Immense Journey* (New York: Time, Inc., 1962), pp. 86-87.

13. In more formal language this is spelled out by Pierre Teilhard de Chardin who spoke of "the fundamental change of view which since the sixteenth century has been steadily exploding and rendering fluid what had seemed to be the ultimate stability—our concept of the world itself. To our clearer vision the universe is no longer a State but a Process. The Cosmos has become a Cosmogenesis. And it may be said without exaggeration that, directly or indirectly, all the intellectual crises through which civilization has passed in the last four centuries arise out of the successive stages whereby a static *Weltanschauung* has been and is being transformed, in our minds and hearts, into a *Weltanschauung* of movement. . . . This is a major event which must lead, as we shall see, to the profound modification of the whole structure not only of our Thought but of our Beliefs"; *The Future of Man*, trans. by Norman Denny (New York: Harper & Row, 1964), pp. 261-62.

14. Albert Camus in his book, *The Rebel: An Essay on Man in Revolt* (A revised and complete translation of *L'Homme Revolte* by Anthony Bower; New York: Vintage Books, 1956), argues that "the murder of the King-priest [Louis XVI, on January 21, 1793] symbolizes the secularization of our history and the disincarnation of the Christian God. Up to now God played a part in history through the medium of the kings. But His representative in history has been

killed, for there is no longer a king. Therefore there is nothing but a semblance of God, relegated to the heaven of principles.

"The revolutionaries may well refer to the Gospel, but in fact they dealt a terrible blow to Christianity, from which it has not yet recovered" (p. 120).

15. John Adams' letter to James Lloyd, dated March 29, 1815: "The last twenty-five years of the last century, and the first fifteen years of this, may be called the age of revolutions and constitutions. We began the dance, and have produced eighteen or twenty models of constitutions, the excellence and defects of which you probably know better than I do. They are, no doubt, the best for us that we could contrive and agree to adopt." In Adrienne Koch, ed., *The American Enlightenment: The Shaping of the American Experiment and a Free Society* (New York: George Braziller, 1965), p. 223.

16. Seymour Martin Lipset, *The First New Nation: the United States in Historical and Comparative Perspective* (New York: Basic Books, Inc., 1963).

17. While using here the word "adapt" I am aware of the subtle differences between "adaptation," "adjustment," and "accommodation" as defined by John Dewey in *A Common Faith* (New Haven: Yale University Press, 1963; pp. 15-17). Religious developments in the United States of course exhibited all three aspects.

18. See, e.g., Michael Novak, *The Experience of Nothingness* (New York: Harper & Row, 1970).

19. Speech to the Republican State Convention in Springfield, Illinois, on June 16, 1858.

20. Erik H. Erikson, *Dimensions of a New Identity: the 1973 Jefferson Lectures in the Humanities* (New York: W. W. Norton & Co., 1974), p. 13.

21. Cappon, ed., *Adams-Jefferson Letters . . .* , p. 525. Adams' letter to Jefferson, dated May 29, 1818.

22. In H. Shelton Smith, Robert T. Handy, and Lefferts A. Loetscher, *American Christianity: an Historical Interpretation with Representative Documents,* I (New York: Charles Scribner's Sons, 1960), p. 58.

23. Perry Miller and Thomas H. Johnson, *The Puritans,* I (New York: Harper & Row Torchbooks, 1963), p. 231.

24. *Letters From an American Farmer* (New York: E.P. Dutton & Co., 1957), pp. 37, 39, 40. The *Letters* were first published in 1782.

In amplification Crèvecoeur continues, "He is an American who, leaving behind him all his ancient prejudices and manners, receives new ones from the new mode of life he has embraced, the new government he obeys, and the new rank he holds. He becomes an American by being received in the broad lap of our great *Alma Mater.* Here individuals of all nations are melted into a new race of men, whose labours and posterity will one day cause great changes in the world. Americans are the western pilgrims, who are carrying along with them that great mass of arts, sciences, vigour, and industry which began long since in the east; they will finish the great circle" (p. 39).

25. In *Benjamin Franklin's Autobiography,* [with] Introduction by Dixon Wecter [and] *Selected Writings,* Edited with an Introduction by Larzer Ziff (New York: Holt, Rinehart and Winston, 1948, 1959), p. 258.

26. James Baldwin, "The Discovery of What It Means to be an American," in *Nobody Knows My Name: More Notes of a Native Son* (New York: Dell Publishing Co., 1961), pp. 17-23.

27. Spenser, *The Faerie Queene,* Book III, Canto v, stanza 43, in Smith and DeSelincourt, eds., *Spenser Poetical Works,* p. 170.

28. I have in mind here the definition of John Courtney Murray: "By pluralism here I mean the co-existence within the one political community of groups that hold divergent and incompatible views with regard to religious questions—those ultimate questions that concern the nature and destiny of man within a universe that stands under the reign of God. Pluralism therefore implies disagreement and dissension within the community. But it also implies a community within which there must be agreement and consensus." In *We Hold These Truths: Catholic Reflections on the American Proposition* (New York: Image Books, 1964), pp. 9-10.

Insofar Murray here left open the question of the relation between disagreement "with regard to . . . ultimate questions" and the basis for "agreement and consensus" in the inclusive community— the heart of the theological issue. George Santayana suggested that in a healthy democracy "fundamental agreement" must be "presupposed" so that "all questions at issue must be minor matters; fundamentals must have been silently agreed upon and taken for granted when the democracy arose"; "English Liberty in America," in *Character and Opinion in the United States* (New York: W. W. Norton & Co., 1967), p. 206. But this does not answer the historical questions of what were the "fundamentals," and by what theology or philosophy were they legitimated so that they came to be "presupposed"?

29. Minersville School District *v.* Gobitis, 310 US 586 (1940), in Joseph Tussman, ed., *The Supreme Court on Church & State* (New York: Oxford University Press, 1962), p. 82.

30. See Joseph L. Blau, "What's American About American Jewry?" in *Judaism: A Quarterly Journal of Jewish Life and Thought,* VII, 3 (Summer, 1958), 2-3.

31. David Freeman Hawks, ed., *Captain John Smith's History of Virginia, A Selection* (Indianapolis: Bobbs-Merrill Co., 1970), pp. xix, 71, 75, 175, 177.

32. "Nicaea, Council of," *Encyclopedia Britannica,* 1959, XVI, 410.

33. Thomas Luckmann, *The Invisible Religion: The Problem of Religion in Modern Society* (New York: Macmillan Co., 1967), p. 107.

And see the editor's "Commentary on the Verse Essays" of John Dryden, in William Frost, ed., *John Dryden Selected Works,* 2nd ed. (New York: Holt, Rinehart and Winston, 1971), p. 228.

34. H. Richard Niebuhr, "The Idea of Covenant and American Democracy," *Church History,* XXIII (June 1954), 128.

For extensive treatment of this theme, see E. M. W. Tillyard, *The Elizabethan World Picture* (New York: Vintage Books, n.d.), *passim.*

For consequent political theories see Walter Ullmann, *Principles of Government and Politics in the Middle Ages* (New York: Barnes & Noble, 1966), *passim;* but especially the Introduction, "The ascending and descending themes of government," pp. 19-26.

35. Alfred North Whitehead, *Essays in Science and Philosophy* (New York: Philosophical Library, 1948), p. 53. The essay in which this occurs, "An Appeal to Sanity," was first published in 1939.

36. I have spelled this out in *The Nation with the Soul of a Church* (New York: Harper & Row, 1975), pp. 111-12, and p. 150, note #67. It is the old problem that John Dryden wrestled with in his *Religio Laici, Or, A Layman's Faith* (1682) and *The Hind and the Panther* (1687); see William Frost, ed., *John Dryden Selected Works,* pp. 227-317.

When the monopolies of Established churches were broken some institutions in the society had to be given power to adjudicate the differences between religious sects that threatened the civil order. The new American Constitution gave this authority to the courts. Always before in Christendom the differences between religious sects were adjudicated by courts in which one of the sects (the Established church) participated. The American way *de-sectarianized* the courts that adjudicated. This did not mean "secularized." The courts defend the right of the private judgment of a sect vis-à-vis all other sects.

37. This theme is expanded in my *The Nation with the Soul of a Church*, p. 30.

38. "Many Mansions," in *American Historical Review*, XLIX, 2 (January, 1964), 315.

39. Pascal's *Pensées*, #22, as in T. S. Eliot, ed., *Pascal's Pensées* (New York: E. P. Dutton & Co., 1958), p. 7.

40. Compare, "The work of the *philosophes* was not only to destroy an old faith, but to supply a new faith, which would be in conformity with the new age, to give a supreme significance to [i.e., to legitimate] the rise of science, the growth of the State and the improvement of civilization. Voltaire spoke for the *philosophes* as a whole when he wrote . . . in 1759 that he had to destroy in order to build. The *philosophes* became the principle spokesmen of a new philosophy of religion which was to be distinctively modern and pragmatic. The impact of this new philosophy altered the position of the Church in the eighteenth century," primarily, I would add, by breaking the churches' monopoly control of "salvation." Charles A. Gliozzo, "The Philosophes and Religion: Intellectual Origins of the Dechristianization Movement in the French Revolution," *Church History*, XL, 3 (September, 1971), 282.

41. Alfred North Whitehead, *Adventures of Ideas*, p. 23.

42. The full text is in Smith, Handy, and Loetscher. *American Christianity*, Vol. I, pp. 328-35. I am aware of the tendential snobbishness of the Harvard group of academics, and that the academic at any time is only with great caution to be equated with the intellectual in society. Academe is indeed for many a bastion against being intellectuals. But this Harvard testimony against Whitefield is a classic statement of the criticisms that have been launched successively against every big-time revivalist in America.

43. Benjamin Franklin's estimation of the quality of Whitefield's discourse and writing makes the point clear. When speaking, said Franklin, Whitefield's "every accent, every emphasis, every modulation of voice, was so perfectly well turned and well placed that, without being interested in the subject, one could not help being pleased with the discourse; a pleasure of much the same kind with that received from an excellent piece of music." But "his writing and printing . . . gave great advantage to his enemies" because of the "unguarded expressions, and even erroneous opinions" which enabled his critics to attack "his writing violently, and with . . . much appearance of reason . . ." So, Franklin concluded, that "if he had never written anything, he would have left behind him a much more numerous and important sect, and his reputation might in that case have been still growing, even after his death . . ." From the *Autobiography* as in Wecter and Ziff, eds., *Benjamin Franklin's Autobiography . . . [and] Selected Writings*, p. 104.

44. Perry Miller, *The Life of the Mind in America from the Revolution to the Civil War* (New York: Harcourt, Brace & World, 1965), p. 202. My argument at this point is greatly indebted to the entire chapter four of this book, "Law and Morality," pp. 186-206.

CHAPTER II

1. "For order does not display itself of itself; if it can be said to be there at all, it is not there for the mere looking. There is no way of pointing a finger or a camera at it; order must be discovered and, in a deep sense, it must be created. What we see, as we see it, is more disorder." J. Bronowski, *Science and Human Values,* rev. ed. (New York: Harper and Row Torchbook, 1965), pp. 13-14.

2. *The Faerie Queene,* Book III, Canto vi, Stanzas 36-39; in *Spenser Poetical Works,* ed. by J. C. Smith and E. DeSelincourt (London: Oxford University Press, 1966).

3. Horace Bushnell, "Preliminary Dissertation [on] Language . . . ," in *God in Christ . . .* (Hartford: Brown and Parsons, 1849), p. 9.

4. Loren Eiseley, *The Immense Journey* (New York: Time, Inc., 1962), p. 88.

5. Ruth Benedict, *Patterns of Culture* (Boston: Houghton Mifflin Co., 1959), p. 2.

6. J. Bronowski, *The Common Sense of Science* (New York: Vintage Books, 1953), p. 78. In amplification Bronowski argues that "if we are to begin at the beginning we must grasp that we are all part of the world we observe. We cannot divide the world into ourselves on one side of the screen as spectators, and everything else as a spectacle on the other side, which we remotely observe. . . . At this point our philosophy must be right"; and as "the most remarkable practical example of this" he notes that "Physicists since Newton have been describing the world as a network of events. But physics does not consist of events: it consists of observations, and between the event and us who observe it there must pass a signal—a ray of light perhaps, a wave or an impulse—which simply cannot be taken out of the observation. This is the insight which Einstein showed in 1905. . . ." (p. 102).

For a popular but instructive explication of this view and its practical consequences see Theodore Roszak, *The Making of a Counter Culture* (Garden City, New York: Doubleday, 1969), esp. Chapter 7, "The Myth of Objective Reality."

7. Eiseley, *The Immense Journey*, p. 87.

8. Here I invoke the conception of "causation in history" developed by R. G. Collingwood in his *An Essay on Metaphysics* (Oxford: The Clarendon Press, 1940), "Part IIIc: Causation," pp. 285-337.

9. "Reality" in the sense developed by Peter L. Berger and Thomas Luckmann, *The Social Construction of Reality* (New York: Anchor Book, Doubleday & Co., 1967), *passim*. Back of this paragraph, and indeed of my whole argument, lies the view delineated by R. G. Collingwood in Part IIIA of his *An Essay on Metaphysics*.

10. For amplification, see "The Fact of Pluralism and the Persistence of Sectarianism," in *The Nation with the Soul of a Church* (New York: Harper & Row, 1975), pp. 48-49; and Chapter I and note #28, above.

11. Philip Schaff, *America: a Sketch of the Political, Social, and Religious Character of the United States of North America, in two Lectures, Delivered at Berlin with a Report Read Before the German*

Diet at Frankfort-am-Maine, September 1854 (Cambridge: Belknap Press, Harvard University, 1961), pp. 71, 81.

12. Peter L. Berger, *Invitation to Sociology: A Humanistic Perspective* (Garden City, New York: Doubleday & Co., 1963), pp. 56-57.

13. This is brilliantly spelled out by Joseph Haroutunian in his article, "Theology and American Experience," in *Criterion* (the erstwhile house organ of the Divinity School of the University of Chicago), III, 1 (Winter, 1964), 3-11. Prof. Bernard E. Meland's commentary on Haroutunian's paper (pp. 11-12) seems to me largely to miss the point.

Lyman Beecher had a strong sense of the implications of this situation—see Chapter V.

14. For amplification see E. M. W. Tillyard, *The Elizabethan World Picture* (New York: Vintage Book, n.d.). Chapters 2 and 4 are especially pertinent.

15. This theme has been extensively developed in recent years. See, for example, Henry Bamford Parkes, *The American Experience: An Interpretation of the History and Civilization of the American People* (New York: Vintage Books, 1959), pp. 193ff.

My version of the general theme is developed in the essay, "The American People: Their Space, Time, and Religion," in *The Lively Experiment: The Shaping of Christianity in America* (New York: Harper & Row, 1963), pp. 1-15.

16. John Tracy Ellis, *American Catholicism*, 2nd ed., rev. (Chicago: University of Chicago Press, 1969), p. 51.

17. Alexis de Tocqueville, *Democracy in America*, trans. by George Lawrence, ed. by J. P. Mayer and Max Lerner, I (New York: Harper & Row, 1966), pp. 51-53.

18. George Herbert Mead, "The Problem of Society: How We Become Selves," in *George Herbert Mead on Social Psychology*, ed. by Anselm Strauss (Chicago: University of Chicago Press, 1964), pp. 20-21.

19. From *Leviathan*, as quoted in *From Absolutism to Revolution 1648-1848*, ed. by Herbert H. Rowen (New York: The Macmillan Co., 1963), pp. 19-21.

20. Karl Jaspers, *The Origin and Goal of History* (New Haven: Yale University Press, 1953), pp. 1-2. See also Henry Bamford

Parkes, *Gods and Men: the Origins of Western Culture* (New York: Vintage Books, 1959), pp. 76-81.

21. Parkes, *Gods and Men,* p. 78.

22. *Ibid.,* p. 81. Loren Eiseley's interpretation is similar: "The story of Eden is a greater allegory than man has ever guessed. For it was truly man who, walking memoryless through bars of sunlight and shade in the morning of the world, sat down and passed a wondering hand across his heavy forehead. Time and darkness, knowledge of good and evil, have walked with him ever since. It is the destiny struck by the clock in the body in that brief space between the beginning of the first ice and that of the second. In just that interval a new world of terror and loneliness appears to have been created in the soul of man." *The Immense Journey,* p. 90.

23. In Deuteronomy 30 man is commanded to choose: "See, today I set before you life and prosperity, death and disaster. If you obey the commandments of Yahweh . . . Yahweh . . . will bless you . . . But if your heart strays . . . if you let yourself be drawn into worshipping other gods and serving them . . . you will certainly perish. . . . I set before you life or death, blessing or curse. Choose life. . . ." It is definitely suggested that this commandment is internalized: "For this Law that I enjoin on you today is not beyond your strength or beyond your reach. It is not in heaven, so that you need to wonder, 'Who will go up to heaven for us and bring it down to us, so that we may hear it and keep it?' Nor is it beyond the seas, so that you need to wonder, 'Who will cross the seas for us and bring it back to us, so that we may hear it and keep it?' No, the Word is very near to you, it is in your mouth and in your heart for your observance." 30:11-20, Jerusalem Bible.

24. Alfred North Whitehead, *Adventures of Ideas* (New York: Free Press, 1967), pp. 18, 55.

25. Parkes, *Gods and Men,* p. 437.

26. Faith E. Burgess, *The Relationship between Church and State according to John Courtney Murray, S. J.* (Dusseldorf: Rudolf Stehle, 1971), p. 121. What John Courtney Murray actually said was that ". . . The voice of America (ironically, a deist and Protestant voice giving a Catholic answer)" to "the great question raised for the first time in the nineteenth century, 'Who are the people?' " (p. 163).

27. See my *The Nation With the Soul of a Church* (New York: Harper & Row, 1975), p. 74.

28. In the "A Bill for Establishing Religious Freedom in Virginia," in Padover, *The Complete Jefferson,* p. 947. This is the version Jefferson introduced into the Virginia Assembly on June 13, 1779. Some changes were made in the version finally passed in 1786.

29. Letter to Adams, June 15, 1813, in Lester Cappon, ed., *The Adams-Jefferson Letters,* p. 331.

30. "The Yeti," in *Atlantic Monthly,* CCXXXVI, 5 (November, 1975), 50.

31. Cappon, ed., *The Adams-Jefferson Letters,* p. 455. Jefferson dated "the dawn of the Revolution in March, 1764"; in Padover, *The Complete Jefferson,* p. 897.

32. Samuel West, "A Sermon Preached before the Honorable Council, and the Honorable House of Representatives of the Colony of Massachusetts Bay, . . . May 29th, 1776," as in Peter Carroll, ed., *Religion and the Coming of the American Revolution* (Waltham, Mass.: Ginn-Blaisdell, 1970), p. 155.

33. Compare John Dewey, "For we are forced to acknowledge that concretely there is no such thing as religion in the singular. There is only a multitude of religions," the argument of chapter one "Religion Versus the Religious," of his book, *A Common Faith* (New Haven: Yale University Press, 1934), p. 7.

34. Philip Schaff, *America . . . ,* p. 88. Schaff continues, "This universal kingship is what the American Republic aims at. Whether it will ever realize it is a very different question. Certainly not by the unfolding of any powers of mere nature. The Bible idea of a general priesthood and kingship can be realized only by supernatural grace, and will not appear in its full reality before the consummation of all things at the glorious coming of Christ." Here Schaff suggests a Christian version of the self-transcending nation.

35. Thomas Luckmann, *The Invisible Religion: The Problem of Religion in Modern Society* (New York: The Macmillan Co., 1967). The quotations are from pp. 117, 116, and 115, in that order.

36. *Ibid.,* pp. 116-17.

37. Raymond Williams, *Culture and Society 1780-1950* (New York: Harper & Row Torchbook, 1966), p. 325.

38. As quoted in Fawn M. Brodie, *Thomas Jefferson: An Intimate History* (Toronto: Bantam Books, 1974), p. 398.

39. Adams to Jefferson, Feb. 2d, 1817, in Lester Cappon, ed., *The Adams-Jefferson Letters,* pp. 506-507.

40. In the fifty-first Federalist Paper, as in Clinton Rossiter, ed., *The Federalist Papers. . . .* (New York: A Mentor Book, 1961), p. 322.

41. Bernard Mandeville, *The Fable of the Bees: or Private Vices, Public Benefits, 1705-1728, passim.*

42. The text of *The Modell . . .* is conveniently accessible in Perry Miller and Thomas H. Johnson, eds., *The Puritans,* I, rev. ed. (New York: Harper & Row Torchbook, 1963), pp. 195-99. For a clear summary of Puritan beliefs, see Ralph Barton Perry, *Puritanism and Democracy* (New York: Vanguard Press, 1944), Chapter 5, ''What Did the Puritans Believe?''

43. As stated in *The Cambridge Platform* of 1648, Chapter I, Section 2, and Chapter II, Section 5. Williston Walker, ed., *The Creeds and Platforms of Congregationalism* (Boston: Pilgrim Press, 1960), pp. 203, 205. Walker's classic was first published in 1893.

44. In sociological terms the nature and structure of such a ''total community'' is spelled out at great length by Thomas Luckmann in his *The Invisible Religion.* My brief reference here assumes acceptance of his thesis and explanation ''for substance thereof.''

In justification of the Massachusetts Bay system to Lord Say and Seal in 1636, John Cotton clearly stated the basic premise of such a commonwealth. ''. . . the word, and scriptures of God,'' he explained, ''doe conteyne a short *upoluposis,* or platforme, not onely of theology, but also of other sacred sciences, . . . attendants, and handmaids thereunto, which he maketh ethicks, eoconomicks, politicks, church-government, prophecy, academy.'' God, he declared, prescribed ''perfect rules'' not only ''for the right ordering of a private man's soule to everlasting blessedness with himselfe, but also for the right ordering of a mans family, yea, of the commonwealth too, so farre as both of them are subordinate to spiritual ends. . . .'' So ''when a commonwealth hath liberty to mould his owne frame . . . I conceyve the scripture hath given full direction for the right ordering of the same. . . .'' Miller and Johnson, *The Puritans,* I, p. 209.

45. Robert Baird, *Religion in America; or, An Account of the Origin, Relation to the State, and Present Condition of the Evangelical Churches in the United States, with Notices of the*

Unevangelical Denominations. This was published in Scotland in
1843, and reprinted in the U.S. the following year. I have used the
1845 edition, published by Harper & Brothers, pp. 99, 59.

46. John Cotton's letter to Lord Say and Seal in 1636, in Miller
and Johnson, eds., *The Puritans,* I, p. 210.

The concept of covenant meant to these Puritans that government
of the Saints must be by consent. As the Cambridge Platform
explains, "The matter of a visibile church are *Saints* by calling,"
and its *"Form* is the *Visible Covenant,* Agreement, or consent
whereby they give up themselves unto the Lord, to the observing of
the ordinances of Christ together in the same society, . . . For we
see not otherwise how members can have *Church-power* one over
another mutually." Chapter IV, Section 3, in Walker, ed., *The
Creeds and Platforms of Congregationalism,* pp. 207-208. It is
important that in transforming their commercial company into a
commonwealth, they were stuck with forms for the government of
the Company as chartered. A Company was a government of laws
under the Charter, membership was by consent, each member had
one vote, the members elected their officers, and had power of
discipline and recall, and might set conditions for membership. In
these respects *the government of the saints was "democratic" in the
modern sense.* The saints, of course, ruled the total community as an
oligarchy—insofar Thomas Jefferson Wertenbaker was right in his
study of *The Puritan Oligarchy* (New York: Charles Scribner's Sons,
1947)—in which the non-saints were merely required to take an oath
of allegiance to the saints' government. When they lost confidence
in their ability to tell the saints from the unregenerate, the "democratic" government of the saints came to include all those in the
commonwealth with proper means and status.

These considerations give content to H. Richard Niebuhr's correct
generalization, that "One of the great common patterns that
guided men in the period when American democracy was formed,
that was present both in their understanding and in their action,
and was used in psychology, sociology and metaphysics as in ethics,
politics and religion, was the pattern of the covenant or of federal
society." "The Idea of Covenant and American Democracy,"
Church History, XXIII (June 1954), 129.

47. Gerhard T. Alexis, "Jonathan Edwards and the Theocratic
Ideal," *Church History,* XXXV (September 1966), 343.

48. Herbert Wallace Schneider, *The Puritan Mind* (New York: Henry Holt and Co., 1930), pp. 106-107.

49. Alexis, "Jonathan Edwards and the Theocratic Ideal," *Church History,* pp. 328-43.

50. Jonathan Edwards, "Religious Affections," in *The Works of President Edwards in Eight Volumes,* IV (Worcester: Isaiah Thomas, 1808), p. 133.

51. As Leonard J. Trinterud noted, this meant, for example, that as early as the period of the Confederation, among Presbyterians "the doctrine of the separation of Church and State came more and more to be held in such a way as to require that the Church be neutral on all issues on which its members were disagreed." *The Forming of an American Tradition: A Reexamination of Colonial Presbyterianism* (Philadelphia: Westminster Press, 1949), p. 260.

52. This is spelled out in detail by Leonard J. Trinterud in his book, *The Forming of an American Tradition.* Trinterud documents, for example, that "The Log College men, defeated by this controlled Church Organization, appealed to the laity. They stated the issue as being for or against any real revival of spiritual and ethical life in the Presbyterian Church. They struck so hard, and loosed such a force in turning a spiritually aroused, but not spiritually disciplined, laity against an apathetic and in some instances morally corrupt clergy, that they well-nigh lost control of the situation" (p. 93). Evidence of the antagonism toward the old orders created by the revivalists is encapsulated in Jacob Green's complaint that in theological education "The method we have been in, has been first to make men gentlemen and then make them preachers; and our candidates have no idea of being gospel ministers without living politely" (p. 202). This was in a letter to Joseph Bellamy in 1775.

53. Horace Bushnell in 1849, although not specifically applying it to the revivals and the Revolution, argued the general principle in his address, "The Founders [of New England] Great in their Unconsciousness." Confessing that he was troubled by some of the implications, he proposed to "set it forth as their special glory . . . that they executed by duty and the stern fidelity of their lives what they never propounded in theory or set up as a mark of attainment. . . ." In the authorship of "those great political and social issues which we now look upon as the highest and crowning distinctions of

our history," Bushnell argued, "the fathers of New England" were "unconscious or undesigning" agents. In *Work and Play,* Vol. I of the Centenary Edition of Horace Bushnell's works (New York: Charles Scribner's Sons, 1903), pp. 127, 128-29.

54. Dixon Wecter and Larzer Ziff, eds., *Benjamin Franklin's Authobiography* and *Selected Writings* (New York: Holt, Rinehart & Winston, 1948 & 1959), p. 77.

55. See, e.g., *The Lively Experiment . . . ,* Chapter III, "American Protestantism During the Revolutionary Epoch," pp. 38-54.

56. This I argued extensively in my dissertation published as *Nathaniel William Taylor 1786-1858: A Connecticut Liberal* (Chicago: University of Chicago Press, 1942); see esp. Chapters IV, VI, and VII.

57. See my article, "The Rise of the Evangelical Conception of the Ministry in America (1607-1850)," in H. Richard Niebuhr and Daniel D. Williams, eds., *The Ministry in Historical Perspectives* (New York: Harper & Bros., 1956), pp. 226-30; 240-42.

58. Ralph E. Morrow, "The Great Revival, the West, and the Crisis of the Church," in John Francis McDermott, ed., *The Frontier Reexamined* (Chicago: University of Chicago Press, 1967), pp. 75-76.

59. In *Church History,* XXXIX, 3 (September, 1970), 345.

Theodore Parker, one of the shrewdest analysts of the social and religious trends of his day, recognized that the orthodox clergy, in contrast to the Unitarians, could and did arouse the genuine religious feeling; yet their "popular theology" tended to funnel it into the "internal glitter" of a sickly and "unnatural mysticism" with no social concern, or, more commonly in New England, into an "ecclesiastical ritualism" of wooden observances—church attendance, Sabbath keeping, Lord's Supper, baptisms, prayer meetings, etc. So the authentic "pious feeling" of the convert in the revivals spends itself "in secreting this abnormal shell of ritualism . . . and has no other influence." It was because Parker thought that the primary effect of conversion in the orthodox revivals thus submerged the convert's sense of social responsibility, that he concluded that "the evil [in them] far surpasses the good." For whether lost in "ecclesiastical ritualism" or "unnatural mysticism," in the ears of such persons "vain are the cries of humanity." Their "ears [are] stuffed with condensed wind" and "their lives are little, dirty, and mean." See Rufus Leighton, ed., *Autobiography, Poems and Prayers by Theodore Parker* (Boston: American Unitarian Association, n.d.), pp. 360-61; and "A False and True Revival of Religion," in George Willis Cooke, ed., *The Transient and Permanent in Christianity by Theodore Parker* (Boston: American Unitarian Association, 1908), p. 387. These volumes are in the Centenary Edition of Parker's works.

60. See Mary Kelley and Sidney E. Mead, "Protestantism in the Shadow of Enlightenment," *Soundings,* LVIII, 3 (Fall, 1975), 335-38.

Jefferson lived to note that "The atmosphere of our country is unquestionably charged with a threatening cloud of fanaticism, lighter in some parts, denser in others, but too heavy in all." Letter to Thomas Cooper, November 2, 1822, in Norman Cousins, ed., *"In God We Trust": The Religious Beliefs and Ideas of the American Founding Fathers* (New York: Harper & Bros., 1958), p. 163.

Henry May, most acute recent student of the American Enlightenment, noted that "Many Americans living in the late eighteenth century believed that they lived in a period more enlightened than those which preceded it. And I have run into a number who sensed the end of this period, people who felt themselves uncomfortable in the age of bible societies, sabbatarian movements, and emotional pre-Jacksonian politics. These are not all stuffy old gentlemen of what Parrington called 'the tie-wig school'; they include for instance both Jefferson and Adams." "The Problem of the American Enlightenment," *New Literary History,* I, 2 (Winter, 1970), 202.

61. Walter Rauschenbusch, *Christianity and the Social Crisis* (New York: The Macmillan Co., 1907). Rauschenbusch argued that "the relation between Christianity and the social crisis is one of the most pressing questions for all intelligent men who realize the power of religion, and most of all for the religious leaders of the people who give direction to the forces of religion" (p. xii). In Part I of his *Christianizing the Social Order* (New York: Macmillan, 1912), Rauschenbusch gave his version of the background and significance of the "great spiritual movement . . . the social awakening" in which he explained that "the new thing" among "people in the churches, who have long been consciously religious . . . is the social

application of their religious life . . . ." which is now being poured
". . . into a broader channel of social purpose, running with a swift
flow toward the achievement of public justice and love" (p. 7). That
this was thought to be a "new thing" in their Christendom would
astounded centuries of professed Christians.

62. *The Christian Century,* LIII (September, 1935), 1168.

CHAPTER III

1. It seems generally accepted that "The Christianity which
developed in the United States was unique. It displayed features
which marked it as distinct from previous Christianity in any other
land." Kenneth Scott Latourette, *A History of the Expansion of
Christianity* (New York: Harper & Brothers, 1937-45), Vol. 4,
p. 424.

2. For definition of "accommodate" as distinct from "adjust"
and "adapt" see John Dewey, *A Common Faith* (New Haven: Yale
University Press, 1963), pp. 15-17.

3. H. Richard Niebuhr was always acutely aware of the problems
pluralism posed for dialogue. For example: "Every effort to deal
with the history of ideas is beset by hazards. Semantic traps are
strewn along the way of the inquirer; such words as democracy,
liberty, justice, etc., point to different concepts or varying complexes
of concepts as they are used in different periods of history and by
different men. The unuttered and frequently unacknowledged
presuppositions of those who employ them also vary; and since
meaning largely depends on context the difficulties of understanding what is meant are increased by the difficulty of ascertaining what
is at the back of the minds. Our hazards are multiplied when the
ideas in question are of a moral and religious sort." "The Idea of
Covenant and American Democracy," *Church History,* XXIII (June
1954), 126.

4. Alexis de Tocqueville, *Democracy in America,* ed. by J. P.
Mayer and Max Lerner; trans. by George Lawrence (New York:
Harper & Row, 1966), Part II, chap. 2, p. 398. Samuel Butler stated
Tocqueville's point succinctly: "So it is with most of us: that which
we observe to be taken as a matter of course by those round us, we
take as a matter of course ourselves." Samuel Butler, *Erewhon, or*

Over the Range (New York: The New American Library of World Literature, 1960), p. 138. The complete *Erewhon* was first published in 1872.

5. *The Broken Covenant: American Civil Religion in Time of Trial* (New York: The Seabury Press, 1975), p. xi.

6. James Baldwin, *Nobody Knows My Name: More Notes of a Native Son* (New York: Dell Publishing Co., 1961), pp. 15-19.

7. Ralph H. Gabriel, *The Course of American Democratic Thought,* 2nd ed. (New York: Ronald Press Co., 1956), p. 13.

8. Ruth Benedict, *Patterns of Culture* (Boston: Houghton Mifflin Co., 1959), p. 16.

9. Edward Shils, "The Intellectuals and the Powers: Some Perspectives for Comparative Analysis," in Philip Rieff, ed., *On Intellectuals* (Garden City, N.Y.: Doubleday & Co., 1970), p. 41.

10. Robin M. Williams, Jr., *American Society: A Sociological Interpretation* (New York: Knopf, 1952), pp. 304 ff.

11. Paul Tillich, *Theology of Culture,* ed. by Robert C. Kimball (New York: Oxford University Press Galaxy Book, 1964), p. 42.

12. Philip Selznick, "Natural Law and Sociology," in John Cogley, Robert M. Hutchins, *et al., Natural Law and Modern Society* (Cleveland: World Publishing Co., 1966), pp. 158, 170.

See also the "Sociological Definition of Religion" developed by Charles Y. Glock and Rodney Stark, *Religion and Society in Tension* (Chicago: Rand McNally & Co., 1965), Chap. 1, pp. 3-17.

13. There is considerable evidence from psychiatrists that whether or not individuals will hold and cherish such beliefs is not a matter of choice, for without them they die. See for example, Viktor E. Frankl, *Man's Search for Meaning: An Introduction to Logotherapy,* originally published as *From Death-Camp to Existentialism* (New York: Washington Square Press, n.d.), Part I, "Experiences in a Concentration Camp," pp. 3-148; Bruno Bettelheim, *The Informed Heart: Autonomy in a Mass Age* (Glencoe, Ill.: The Free Press, 1960), *passim,* but esp. chap. 4, 5; Robert Jay Lifton, *Revolutionary Immortality: Mao Tse-Tung and the Chinese Cultural Revolution* (New York: Random House Vintage Books, 1968).

14. Alfred North Whitehead, "An Appeal to Sanity," in *Essays in Science and Philosophy* (New York: Philosophical Library, 1948), pp. 55-56.

15. I am using the words *presupposed,* and *presupposition(s)*— for substance thereof at least—with the meaning and connotations

developed by R. G. Collingwood in *An Essay on Metaphysics* (Oxford: Clarendon Press, 1940), pp. 21-48.

16. For this reason one cannot understand believers simply by listening to what they profess. We are all Erewhonians in this respect: "It is a distinguishing peculiarity of the Erewhonians that when they profess themselves to be quite certain about any matter, and avow it as a base on which they are to build a system of practice, they seldom quite believe in it. If they smell a rat about the precincts of a cherished institution, they will always stop their noses to it if they can." So, the inadvertent visitor concluded, ". . . they did not know themselves what they believed; all they did know was that it was a disease not to believe as they did." That is a good description of the sectarian mind. Samuel Butler, *Erewhon, or Over the Range,* p. 138.

17. Edward Shils, "The Intellectuals and the Powers: . . . ," p. 29.

18. Compare John Dewey, *A Common Faith* (New Haven: Yale University Press, 1934), pp. 9-10: "There is no such thing as religion in the singular. There is only a multitude of religions. 'Religion' is a strictly collective term . . ." (p. 7). ". . . the adjective 'religious' denotes nothing in the way of a specifiable entity, either institutional or as a system of beliefs. It does not denote anything to which one can specifically point to this and that historic religion or existing church."

19. The Modern Library edition, p. 84.

20. Ruth Benedict, *Patterns of Culture,* p. 7.

21. For the imagery of "autobiography" and "biography" I am indebted to William A. Clebsch's book, *From Sacred to Profane America: the Role of Religion in American History* (New York: Harper and Row, 1968), p. 4.

22. H. Richard Niebuhr, *The Meaning of Revelation* (New York: Macmillan Co., 1946), pp. 81-90. Implied in Niebuhr's view is a defense of his species of Christian faith by removing it from the critical scrutiny of the "external" community. Insofar he stood in the tradition of Jonathan Edwards.

23. Jonathan Edwards, "Religious Affections," in *The Works of President Edwards in Eight Volumes* (Worcester, Mass.: Isaiah Thomas, 1808), Vol. IV, p. 134.

24. "The Historian's Vocation," in *Theology Today,* XIX (April 1962), 75-89.

25. John Dewey, *A Common Faith,* p. 9.

26. Ruth Benedict, *Patterns of Culture,* p. 8.

27. Talcott Parsons, "The Intellectual: A Social Role Category," in Philip Rieff, ed., *On Intellectuals,* p. 3.

28. Ibid. John Higham seems to combine features of Parsons' "cultural systems" and "social systems" in his concept of "ideologies" which, he says, are "those explicit systems of general beliefs that give large bodies of people a common identity and purpose, a common program of action, and a standard for self-criticism. Being relatively formalized and explicit, ideology contrasts with a wider, older, more ambiguous fund of myth and tradition. It includes doctrines or theories on the one hand and policies or prescriptions on the other. Accordingly, it links social action with fundamental beliefs, collective identity with the course of history. . . . Arising in the course of modernization when an unreflective culture fractures, ideology provides a new basis for solidarity." "Hanging Together: Divergent Unities in American History," *Journal of American History,* LXI, 1 (June, 1974), 10.

29. Compare another form of this thesis found in John H. Randall, Sr. and John H. Randall, Jr., *Religion and the Modern World* (New York: Stokes Co., 1929), Chapter II, "The Religious Heritage of the Nineteenth Century," pp. 23-44.

30. Actually this seems to me to be commonly recognized as, for example, in the assertion made by Robert M. Brown that Christianity is not where the "greatest decisions" are made. *The Ecumenical Revolution: An Interpretation of the Catholic-Protestant Dialogue* (Garden City, N. Y.: Doubleday & Co., 1967), p. 307.

31. Alfred North Whitehead, *Essays in Science and Philosophy,* pp. 55-56.

For a powerful use of the mainspring figure, see Adlai Stevenson, "Our Broken Mainspring," in Gerry G. Brown, ed., *Adlai E. Stevenson: a Short Biography* (New York: Barron's Educational Series, 1965), pp. 201-15.

32. For example, in Dean M. Kelley's study, *Why Conservative Churches are Growing: A Study in Sociology of Religion* (New York: Harper & Row, 1972), *passim.*

33. "Whatever Happened to Theology," *Christianity and Crisis,* 35, 8 (May 12, 1975). In this issue twelve eminent theologians address this question. Although they differ considerably in explanations of why it happened and when, all seem to agree that theology has disappeared. Among the most enlightening reasons given is that by Rosemary Ruether: ". . . I believe that the demise of such systematic theology is not recent but has been in preparation since the Enlightenment. The attempt to rebuild systematic dogmatics since the 19th century has finally fallen through" (p. 109). Gordon K. Kaufman lamented that "the once proud queen of the sciences, having lost a sense of her own meaning and integrity, had become a common prostitute" (p. 111), catering to a series of fads.

34. Michael Novak, "The Enlightenment is Dead," in *The Center Magazine,* IV (March / April, 1971), 19-20. The title of the article seemed to me to be contradicted by its content, as the quotations suggest.

35. Martin E. Marty, *The New Shape of American Religion* (New York: Harper & Bros., 1958-1959), pp. 71-72.

36. George Herbert Mead, "The Philosophies of Royce, James, and Dewey in Their American Setting," in Andrew J. Reck, ed., *Selected Writings of George Herbert Mead* (Indianapolis: Bobbs-Merrill Company's Library of Liberal Arts, 1964). The quotations are in order from pages 383, 376, 377, 381. The essay was first published in the *International Journal of Ethics,* XL (1929-1930), 211-31. It seems to me that George Santayana argued essentially the same thesis in his famous essay on "The Genteel Tradition."

Herbert Wallace Schneider spelled out "how philosophy [in America] lost its living connections with the general culture of the American people and became a technical discipline in academic curricula. At the same time . . . religion and morals gradually severed their philosophical bonds, and, as the philosophers would say, became unenlightened." *A History of American Philosophy* (New York: Columbia University Press, 1946), p. 225.

37. *Ibid.,* p. 381.

38. Joseph Haroutunian, "Theology and American Experience," *Criterion* (Winter, 1964), pp. 7-9. *Criterion* is, or was, the house organ of the Divinity School of The University of Chicago.

39. Edward Shils, "The Intellectuals and the Powers: . . . ," in Philip Rieff, ed., *On Intellectuals,* pp. 27-30.

Adolf A. Berle, Jr., in his book *Power Without Property: a New Development in American Political Economy* (New York: Harcourt . . . Harvest Book, 1929), e.g., pp. 90-91, 110-16, and 154-55; makes a helpful distinction between the "public consensus" and the "public opinion" that carries the same connotations as Shils' designation of the role of the intellectual vis-à-vis the general population. Berle's "public consensus" points to Shils' "common standards," and his "public opinion" points to temporary winds of opinion which often run counter to the "public consensus" or the "common standards."

In my terminology, developed in articles and unpublished lectures during the past years, the intellectuals define, describe, and teach the elements of the historical "character" of a people who constitute a community, as distinct from the temporary "shapes" their movements may take. A people's conception of their true "character" is invoked in judgment on their immediate "shape."

40. David W. Noble, *Historians Against History: The Frontier Thesis and the National Covenant in American Historical Writing Since 1890,* (Minneapolis: University of Minnesota Press, 1965), pp. 4, 17.

Robert N. Bellah, a self-confessed ". . . former establishment fundamentalist," definitely assumes this role in his book, *The Broken Covenant: American Civil Religion in Time of Trial* (New York: Seabury Press, Crossroad Book, 1975). His "Confessions of a Former Establishment Fundamentalist" was published in *Bulletin of the Council on the Study of Religion,* I, 3 (December, 1970), 3-6.

41. For this distinction, see Tocqueville's "The Principle of the Sovereignty of the People in America," which is Chapter 4 in Vol. I, Part 1 of his *Democracy in America;* in the new translation by George Lawrence and edited by J. P. Mayer and Max Lerner (New York: Harper & Row, 1966), pp. 51-53.

42. This seems to be commonly assumed by historians. For example, Edmund S. Morgan says that the founders of New England "knew, from the works of theologians, what principles they must embody in their new institutions." *Roger Williams: the Church and the State* (New York: Harcourt, Brace & World, 1967), p. 68.

43. See John Neville Figgis, *The Divine Right of Kings* (New York: Harper & Row, Torchbook, 1965), *passim.*

44. See note 36 above. Adams commonly made a distinction between the Revolution and the War for Independence. On May 29, 1818 he wrote, "But what do we mean by the American Revolution? Do we mean the American war? The Revolution was effected before the war commenced. The Revolution was in the minds and hearts of the people; a change in their religious sentiments of their duties and obligations." And this Revolution, he thought, might be said to have begun "as early as the first plantation of the country." Adrienne Koch, ed., *The American Enlightenment: The Shaping of the American Experiment and a Free Society* (New York: George Braziller, 1965), pp. 228, 229.

45. Jefferson was very conscious of the distinction, and in this respect quite aware of how he and his fellow Americans differed from Locke. In his "Notes on Religion" written around 1776 he notes that "Locke denies toleration to those who entertain opinions contrary to those moral rules necessary for the preservation of society; as for instance, that faith is not to be kept with those of another persuasion, that Kings excommunicated forfeit their crowns, that dominion is founded in grace, or that obedience is due to some foreign prince, or who will not own and teach the duty of tolerating all men in matters of religion, or who deny the existence of a god [it was a great thing to go so far—as he himself says of the parliament who framed the act of toleration, but where he stopped short we may go on]." In Saul K. Padover, ed., *The Complete Jefferson. . . .* (New York: Duell, Sloan & Pearce, Inc., 1943), p. 945.

Adrienne Koch, after quoting this in part, adds "That he went on, and America went on, from toleration to religious freedom is very much to the point in our general understanding of the American Enlightenment"; in "Pragmatic Wisdom and the American Enlightenment," *The William and Mary Quarterly*, XVIII, 3 (July 1961), 323.

It seems generally agreed that the American leaders' ideas were not original. Herbert W. Schneider in his *A History of American Philosophy* (p. 36), assents that they "had no systems of thought, and they consciously borrowed most of the scattered ideas which they put into action." One cannot, he argued, "make the American Enlightenment appear as a 'glorious revolution' in thought as well as in fact. . . ."

It seems equally agreed that the Americans differed from the European thinkers because of their practical political experience and their unique opportunity to put the revolutionary ideas into practice. This is stressed by Hannah Arendt *(On Revolution* [New York: Viking Press, 1965], pp. 115-16), who argues that "Compared to this American experience, the preparation of the French *hommes de lettres* who were to make the Revolution was theoretical in the extreme. . . . They had no experience to fall back upon, only ideas and principles untested by reality. . . ."

Adrienne Koch stresses the same point in the Introduction to her *The American Enlightenment,* pp. 19-45.

46. Letter to H. Niles, February 13, 1818, in Adrienne Koch, *The American Enlightenment,* p. 228.

47. The case of Lucy Mack Smith, mother of the prophet, Joseph Smith, illustrates this. See my *The Nation with the Soul of a Church* (New York: Harper and Row, 1975), p. 42, n. 45.

48. Franklin's letter to David Hartley, December 4, 1789, in Adrienne Koch, *The American Enlightenment,* p. 107.

49. In making this point in class lectures Professor Wilhelm Pauck used to tell us that modern man stands either with one foot in the Reformation and the other on a banana peel, or with one foot in the Enlightenment and the other on the banana peel. I suppose that the two most prestigious representatives of the Reformation and the Enlightenment in my day were Karl Barth and Albert Schweitzer respectively.

50. For extensive development of this thesis see John H. Randall, Sr. and John H. Randall, Jr., *Religion and the Modern World* (New York: Stokes Co., 1929); especially Chapter II, "The Religious Heritage of the Nineteenth Century," pp. 23-44.

51. This was extensively spelled out in my *Nathaniel William Taylor: A Connecticut Liberal* (Chicago: University of Chicago Press, 1942), Chapters IV and VI. More recent literature is noted in the article by Mary Kelley and myself, "Protestantism in the Shadow of Enlightenment," *Soundings,* LVIII 3 (Fall, 1975), 345, n. 42.

In Chapter IV below I note Robert Baird's and Horace Bushnell's treatment of Thomas Jefferson which, I think, may fairly be characterized as character assassination.

52. In the Preface to Part II of *The Age of Reason.*

53. See Martin E. Marty, *The Infidel: Free Thought and American Religion* (Cleveland: World Pub. Co.'s Meridian Books, 1961), *passim,* for delineation of how the image of "the infidel" was often created and universally used by Christian leaders in America to rally support for their enterprises by pointing to a common enemy.

54. A striking example of this effect was noted in *Liberty,* LVIII (November-December, 1963), 8-9. In the state of Hawaii Christmas and Good Friday were paid holidays for state employees. This cost the state about $500,000 a year. In February 1963 a state senator introduced two bills into the Hawaiian Legislature. The first would remove Christmas and Good Friday from the list of *paid* holidays. The second, an alternate bill, would add a "Buddha Day" (April 8) to the paid holidays at a cost of about $250,000. It would seem that either bill would be fair, granted the large Buddhist population, and in principle compatible with the Court's interpretation of the First Amendment. But in reaction Protestant Billy Graham declared that "If we take away these days (Christmas and Good Friday), we are taking away the basis of our way of life, our religion," and a Roman Catholic Monsignor asserted that "The state of Hawaii and the other forty-nine states ought to be amazed at the arrogance of those who insult God-fearing people by stamping out the traditional observance of the greatest Christian feast of the year." Obviously neither bill, if passed, would have *taken away,* or *stamped out* either Christmas or Good Friday. What both of these highly visible Christian leaders were actually contending for was continued recognition and support of their species of Christianity by the civil authority and against those of other religious faiths—a direct attack on the principle of religious freedom inherent in the First Amendment.

55. See Chapter IV, p. 94.

56. H. Richard Neibuhr is an example of a very honest, tender and sensitive person and most able thinker impaled on the horns of the dilemma posed by the Christian absolutism he inherited and defended in his denomination and the relativism of the pluralistic cosmopolitan society in which he came to live as a Yale professor. In him the problem of how to be an absolutist in a relativistic and cosmopolitan world; or, vocationally, how to be a theologian for his species of Christianity while a professorial intellectual at pluralistic Yale. My impression is that a majority of professors in the "liberal"

theological schools circumvent this problem by quietly renouncing responsibility for and to the denomination with which they may be at least nominally affiliated. H. Richard Niebuhr was made of sterner mental and spiritual stuff, so in his writings the tension is made manifest.

57. Herbert W. Schneider noted the metamorphosis of the eighteenth-century type of philosopher who was an investigator, either natural or moral into ''the nineteenth-century . . . species of educator known as professors of philosophy'' who ''were primarily teachers'' whose ''ambition was to be orthodox, to teach the truth, i.e., to instruct their students in correct doctrine. . . . Similarly,'' Schneider adds, ''the theologians lost most of their speculative or philosophical interest and were content to refine their systems for the edification of the faithful and the confounding of rival theologians. In short, our history of American philosophy now takes us into the schoolrooms of colleges and seminaries. What President Francis Wayland said of his own famous textbook in moral science states the idea of orthodoxy in general: 'Being designed for the purposes of instruction, its aim is to be simple, clear, and purely didactic.' '' *A History of American Philosophy,* p. 226.

A. N. Whitehead concluded that ''theology has largely failed'' in its function ''to provide a rational understanding of the rise of civilization, and of the tenderness of mere life itself, in a world which superficially is founded upon the clashings of senseless compulsion,'' and stated his belief that ''the defect of the liberal theology of the last two hundred years is that it has confined itself to the suggestion of minor, vapid reasons why people should continue to go to church in the traditional fashion.'' *Adventures of Ideas* (New York: The Free Press, 1967), p. 170.

More devastating was the curt comment of top-flight theologian John B. Cobb, Jr., in 1967 that, while ''there is no lack of highly trained and intelligent men keenly interested in constructive theological work,'' their ''essays for the most part are trivial'' and leave ''a vacuum in which even the splash of a small pebble attracts widespread attention''—and, he should have added, only in the very restricted circle of the jet-set professorial theologians outside of which the attention attracted seems to be practically nil. ''From Crisis Theology to the Post-Modern World,'' in Bernard Murchland, ed., *The Meaning of the Death of God: Protestant, Jewish and*

Catholic Scholars Explore Atheistic Theology (New York: Vintage Books, 1967), p. 138.

58. See Mary Kelley and Sidney E. Mead, "Protestantism in the Shadow of Enlightenment," pp. 338-42.

59. John C. Bennett, "After Liberalism—What?" *The Christian Century,* L (November 8, 1933), 1403.

CHAPTER IV

1. I have been saying this for a long time, perhaps too long. See, e.g., *The Lively Experiment* . . . (New York: Harper and Row, 1963), Chapter 4, pp. 55-71, and *passim.*

2. Reference is to the article by Crane Brinton, "Many Mansions," in *American Historical Review,* XLIX, 2 (January, 1964), 315; noted above in Chapter I, p. 28. This to me is a most important point, central to my interpretation of the present situation and how we got this way.

3. "The elements of liberal democratic thought," Herbert McClosky argued, "are not nearly so vague as they are sometimes made out to be, and their coalescence into a single body of belief is by no means fortuitous. American democratic 'Ideology' possesses an elaborately defined theory, a body of interrelated assumptions, axioms, and principles, and a set of ideals that serve as guides for action. Its tenets, postulates, sentiments, and values inspired the great revolutions of the seventeenth and eighteenth centuries, and have been repeatedly and explicitly set forth in fundamental documents, such as the Constitution, the Declaration, and the Federalist Papers." McClosky then lists what he thinks "scholars or Supreme Court justices . . . would uniformly recognize as elements of American democratic ideology." "Consensus and Ideology in American Politics," *American Political Science Review,* LVIII (June, 1964), 362-63.

Frank Freidel in his Preface to Adrienne Koch's *The American Enlightenment* (New York: George Braziller, 1965) notes that "Out of the classic period of American thought, the age of the Enlightenment, came a body of ideas which, incorporated in our constitutions and our political traditions, have served as fundamental guidelines for the nation throughout its history. These principles, embodied in such documents as the Declaration of Independence, the Constitution, and the Bill of Rights, have retained their cogency through the centuries.''

Herbert W. Schneider held that ''the American Enlightenment . . . contains the heart of our heritage as a people and our deepest ties to the rest of humanity.'' *A History of American Philosophy* (New York: Columbia University Press, 1946), p. 22.

Michael Novak's persuasive argument that Enlightenment is ''the dominant religion'' today, and ''the tradition in which intellectuals ordinarily define themselves'' has been noted, Chapter III, p. 71.

4. *Religion in America: An Historical Account of the Development of American Religious Life,* 2nd ed. (New York: Charles Scribner's Sons, 1973), p. 92.

I think Hudson is wrong in saying that there was ''nothing distinctively Christian'' about, for example, the dogmas Benjamin Franklin said he ''never doubted, for instance, the existence of the Deity; that he made the world, and govern'd it by his Providence; that the most acceptable service of God was the doing good to man; that our souls are immortal; and that all crime will be punished, and virtue rewarded here or hereafter.'' In Frank Luther Mott and Chester E. Jorgenson, eds., *Benjamin Franklin; Representative Selections . . .* (New York: American Book Co., 1936), pp. 69-70.

5. The Christian insider is commonly handicapped in discussing alternative perspectives because he has but two categories—things are either ''Christian'' and good, or ''not Christian'' and bad. This simple either/or classification which Hudson exhibits here, slights, even ignores, the complexity of historical positions. In contrast one may note Charles A. Gliozza's characterization of Rousseau's religion as including ''theism with reminiscences of Christianity,'' to which he adds examples of Rousseau's ''Christian spirit.'' ''The Philosophes and Religion: Intellectual Origins of the Dechristianization Movement in the French Revolution,'' *Church History,* XL, 3 (September, 1971), 279.

6. Arthur W. Peach, ed., *Selections from the Works of Thomas Paine* (New York: Harcourt, Brace, 1928), p. 346.

Just a year and a half before he died Jefferson called himself a Unitarian, who because of his situation ''must therefore be contented to be a Unitarian by myself.'' Quoted in Adrienne Koch, *The Philosophy of Thomas Jefferson* (Chicago: Quadrangle Books Paperback, 1964), p. 27.

John Dewey's characterization of Jefferson as "a sincere theist" seems amply documented by even casual perusal of his writings. Dewey continues, that "although his rejection of supernaturalism and of the authority of churches and their creeds caused him to be denounced as an atheist, he was convinced beyond any peradventure, on natural and rational grounds of the existence of a divine righteous Creator who manifested his purposes in the structure of the world, especially in that of society and human conscience. The equality of all human beings was not psychological nor legal. It was intrinsically moral, as a consequence of the equal moral relation all human beings sustain to their Creator—equality of moral claims and of moral responsibilities." *The Living Thoughts of Thomas Jefferson Presented by John Dewey* (New York: Premier Books, Fawcett World Library, 1960), p. 33.

Jefferson so emphasized the absolute uniqueness of the pure moral system taught by Jesus as to give it an aura of divine revelation.

7. A common tendency to see the American Enlightenment in the context of the French, plus the lasting effect of the success of clerical leaders in imposing the designation "atheist" on Jefferson *et al.* during the Second Great Awakening, has obscured this important difference between American and French leaders and Revolutions.

Jefferson observed in 1814 that "generally, . . . while in Protestant countries the defection from the Platonic Christianity of the priests is to Deism, in Catholic countries they are to Atheism" (Letter to Thomas Law dated June 13, 1814, in Saul K. Padover, *The Complete Jefferson. . . .* [New York: Duell, Sloan & Pearce, 1943], p. 1032). The English colonies were strongly Protestant, and while "Enlightenment" perspective prevailed among the intellectuals, atheists were practically unknown. This is probably the primary reason why, as Adrienne Koch noted, that while the American leaders "staunchly defended the principle of majority rule, they did not make a mystique of the unitary will of the nation out of it" ("Pragmatic Wisdom and the American Enlightenment," *William and Mary Quarterly*, XVIII, [July 1961], 326), as did leaders in France (see Albert Camus, *The Rebel*, trans. by Anthony Bower [New York: Vintage Books, 1956]).

It was the American's retention of the transcendent that made all the difference between what John Courtney Murray designated as

"Jacobin democracy and Anglo-Saxon democracy, or between 'the sovereignty of the people' in the sense of '89 and 'government of the people, for the people, and by the people' in the sense of Lincoln." "The Problem of State Religion," in *Theological Studies,* XII, 2 (June, 1951), 164. Murray designated the "absolutist state-monism" of the former as "laic" or "laicized" and " 'the liberal tradition' " of the West, as "lay" democracy. "Contemporary Orientations of Catholic Thought on Church and State in the Light of History," *Theological Studies,* X, 2 (June, 1949), 226.

"The brand of deism" of Jefferson and most of the Americans "was definitely English in orientation, rather than French" as Adrienne Koch argued. *The Philosophy of Thomas Jefferson* (Chicago: Quadrangle Books, 1964), p. 27.

8. *The Age of Reason,* in Arthur W. Peach, ed., *Selections from the Works of Thomas Paine* (New York: Harcourt, Brace, 1928), pp. 250-51.

9. In Lester J. Cappon, ed., *The Adams-Jefferson Letters,* Vol. II, 1812-1826 (Chapel Hill: University of North Carolina Press, 1959), p. 373.

Back of this paragraph, and indeed of my whole argument, lies the view delineated by R. G. Collingwood in Part IIIA of his *An Essay on Metaphysics* (Oxford: Clarendon Press, 1940).

10. "Isaac Backus and the Separation of Church and State in America," *American Historical Review,* LXXIII (June 1968), 1404.

11. In "A Memorial and Remonstrance on the Religious Rights of Man," as in Joseph L. Blau, ed., *Cornerstones of Religious Liberty in America,* rev. ed. (New York: Harper & Row, 1964), p. 84.

The test of this position is the ability to entertain the possibility that one might be wrong even in matters of life and death. Franklin stated this in the final word of his "Dialogue Between Two Presbyterians": "In the present weak State of humane Nature, surrounded as we are on all sides with Ignorance and Error, it little becomes poor fallible Man to be positive and dogmatical in his Opinions . . . since 'tis an Uncertainty till we get to Heaven what true Orthodoxy in all points is. . . ." In Adrienne Koch, *The American Enlightenment,* p. 118.

Franklin exemplified the position in his plea for acceptance of the Constitution, saying ". . . I consent, Sir, to this Constitution, because I expect no better, and because I am not sure that it is not the best, [and] . . . I . . . wish, that every member of the Convention who may still have objections to it, would with me on this occasion doubt a little of his own infallibility. . . .'' *Ibid.,* pp. 144-45.

Similarly John Adams in discussing theories of power, readily admitted, ''I may be deceived as much as any of them'' who have different views. *The Adams-Jefferson Letters . . . ,* Vol. II, 463.

12. In his ''Notes on Religion'' Jefferson stated the principle clearly: ''The care of every man's soul belongs to himself. . . . The magistrate has no power but what the people gave. The people have not given him the care of souls because they could not, they could not, because no man has *right* to abandon the care of his salvation to another.'' In Padover, *The Complete Jefferson,* pp. 943-44.

13. In Lester J. Cappon, ed., *The Adams-Jefferson Letters . . . ,* Vol. II, 1812-1826. (Chapel Hill: University of North Carolina Press, 1959), p. 608.

To Adams and Jefferson, as to most of the American leaders, the ''substance and essence of Christianity'' was the same as that of all religions—the famous ''essentials of every religion'' as Franklin called them. These men saw clearly that one could not speak religiously to pluralistic America in sectarian terms. In explaining an answer he gave to an ''Army of fine young Fellows'' among whom were ''Roman Catholicks, English Episcopalians, Scotch and American Presbyterians, Methodists, Moravians, Anabaptists, German Lutherans, German Calvinists[,] Universalists, Arians, Priestleyans, Socinians, Independents, Congregationalists, Horse Protestants and House Protestants, Deists and Atheists; and . . . 'Protestants who believe nothing' '' Adams said he could appeal to them only on the basis of ''the general Principles of Christianity, in which all those Sects were United: And the *general Principles* of English and American Liberty, in which all those young Men United. . . .'' Adams avowed ''I then believed, and now believe, that those general Principles of Christianity, are as eternal and immutable, as the Existence and Attributes of God; and that those Principles of Liberty, are as unalterable as human Nature and our terrestrial, mundane System.'' *Ibid.,* pp. 339-40.

14. By forms here is meant organizations, rituals, theological systems. The latter are essentially pictures of God, of the kind suggested in the folklore story of the little boy drawing a picture. When asked what he was drawing he said, ''A picture of God.'' But, protested his mother, ''No one knows what God looks like.'' ''They will when I get through,'' the boy asserted.

15. In 1816 Jefferson wrote, "I have ever judged of the religion of others by their lives . . . for it is in our lives and not from our words, that our religion must be read." Padover, *The Complete Jefferson,* p. 955. A few months later he wrote to John Adams, that he had told a biographer "say nothing of my religion. It is known to my god and myself alone. It's [*sic*] evidence before the world is to be sought in my life. If that has been honest and dutiful to society, the religion which has regulated it cannot be a bad one." Cappon, ed., *The Adams-Jefferson Letters,* II, p. 506.

Franklin in his "Dialogue Between Two Presbyterians" summed up his belief: "I understand it to be the Will of God, that we should live virtuous, upright, and good-doing Lives; as the Prophet understood it, when he said, What doth the Lord require of thee, O Man, but to do justly, love Mercy, and walk humbly with the Lord thy God." Faith, he argued, "is recommended as a Means of producing Morality: Our Saviour was a Teacher of Morality or Virtue, and they that were deficient and desired to be taught, ought first to believe in him as an able and faithful Teacher. Thus Faith would be a Means of producing Morality, and Morality of Salvation. But that from such Faith alone Salvation may be expected, appears to me to be neither a Christian Doctrine nor a reasonable one. . . . Morality or Virtue is the End, Faith only a Means to obtain that End: And if the End be obtained, it is no matter by what Means. . . ." In Adrienne Koch, *The American Enlightenment,* p. 115.

In 1816 John Adams asserted that "my morall or religious Creed, . . . has [been] for 50 or 60 Years . . . contained in four short Words 'Be just and good.' " This he thought was what all religious teaching boiled down to. This result, Jefferson thought in reply, "is that in which all our enquiries must end." Cappon, ed., *Adams-Jefferson Letters,* pp. 449, 506.

16. In "Natural Religion and Religious Liberty in America," *The Journal of Religion,* XXV (January 1945), 54-55.

17. This theme, of course, has a long history in Christendom. In America the progeny include Joseph Priestley's two-volume *History of the Corruptions of Christianity* (Birmingham: J. Thompson, 1793), and highly regarded by Jefferson; and Kirby Page's *Jesus or Christianity* (Garden City, N.Y.: Doubleday Doran & Co., 1929), which had its vogue in the 1930s.

18. In *Notes on the State of Virginia,* Query xvii, in Padover, *The Complete Jefferson,* 676.

19. F. C. S. Schiller, "Pragmatism, Humanism, and Religion" (first pub. 1929), in *Must Philosophers Disagree? and Other Essays in Popular Philosophy* (London: Macmillan & Co., 1934), p. 319.

20. The bill was first introduced into the Virginia Assembly in 1779 but so opposed that it was not adopted, with minor changes, until 1786. Padover, *The Complete Jefferson,* pp. 946-47.

21. In *Notes On the State of Virginia,* Query xvii, in Padover, *The Complete Jefferson,* 675-76.

Jefferson repeated this sentiment many times. In 1815 he wrote, "Difference of opinion leads to inquiry, and inquiry to truth; and that, I am sure, is the ultimate and sincere object of us both." Padover, *The Complete Jefferson,* p. 954.

Again, "I am pleased, however, to see the efforts of hypothetical speculation, because by the collisions of different hypotheses, truth may be elicited and science advance in the end" in John Dewey, ed., *The Living Thoughts of Thomas Jefferson* (New York: Fawcett World Library, 1957), p. 15.

Franklin, speaking of "The Internal State of America" in 1785, noted that "There are parties and discords" but "such will exist wherever there is liberty; and perhaps they help to preserve it. By the collision of different sentiments, sparks of truth are struck out, and political light is obtained" in Adrienne Koch, *The American Enlightenment,* p. 141.

Jefferson concluded that "Nothing but free argument, raillery and even ridicule will preserve the purity of religion" in Padover, *The Complete Jefferson,* p. 939.

This view was apparently quite widespread and clearly expressed by several Independent Divines in England in the 1640s, as Winthrop S. Hudson has made clear in his article, "Denominationalism as a Basis for Ecumenicity: a Seventeenth Century Conception," *Church History,* XXIV (1955), 32-51. As one of them put it, "Sparks are beaten out by the flints striking together. Many sparks of light, many truths, are beaten out by the beatings of men's spirits one against another," p. 40. The words are so nearly alike that one wonders if Franklin had learned them from his seventeenth-century predecessor.

In the thinking of the founders this was a, perhaps the, primary premise of the Republic they envisaged. Madison stated it clearly in the fifty-first Federalist Paper: "In a free government the security for civil rights must be the same as that for religious rights. It consists in the one case in the multiplicity of interests, and in the other in the multiplicity of sects. The degree of security in both cases will depend on the number of interests and sects; . . ."

22. See John H. Randall, Sr., and John H. Randall, Jr., *Religion and the Modern World* (New York: Frederick A. Stokes Co., 1929), pp. 27-28.

23. William A. Clebsch, *From Sacred to Profane America: the Role of Religion in American History* (New York: Harper & Row, 1968), p. 65.

24. This is spelled out in my article, "The Rise of the Evangelical Conception of the Ministry in America (1607-1850)," in H. Richard Niebuhr and Daniel D. Williams, eds., *The Ministry in Historical Perspectives* (New York: Harper & Bros., 1956), pp. 207-49.

25. *The Northern Baptist Convention Annual,* 1908, pp. 25-27.

26. Compare Christianity's record vis-à-vis freedom in the modern world as traced by Herbert J. Muller in *Religion and Freedom in the Modern World* (Chicago: University of Chicago Press, 1963). It has played, Muller argues, "an ambiguous role," on the one hand doing "more to promote the growth of freedom than did any other of the higher religions," but, on the other hand, exhibiting prolonged opposition to "the movements toward popular government, civil liberties, and social reform" (pp. 3-4).

27. There is of course a vast literature on the subject displaying many different emphases and interpretations. My views are summarized in chapter III of *The Lively Experiment . . . ,* (New York: Harper and Row, 1963), pp. 38-54, entitled "American Protestantism During the Revolutionary Epoch." See also my review of Alan Heimert's *Religion and the American Mind from the Great Awakening to the Revolution* in the *Journal of Religion,* XLVIII, 3 (July, 1968) for summary comments on methods and emphases.

28. Erik H. Erikson, *Dimensions of a New Identity: the 1973 Jefferson Lectures in the Humanities* (New York: W. W. Norton & Co., 1974), p. 12.

29. William G. McLoughlin, *Isaac Backus and the American Pietistic Tradition* (Boston: Little Brown & Co., 1967), p. ix.

30. William G. McLoughlin, "Isaac Backus and the Separation of Church and State in America," *American Historical Review,* LXXIII (June, 1968), 1392-1413.

The important differences for the future, McLoughlin argues, were those between what he calls the "rationalist-humanist" premises of Jefferson and Madison and "the evangelical view of Separationism" stemming from Backus *et al*. I agree with McLoughlin's "rationalist" characterization of Jefferson, but think he is badly mistaken if he means by "humanist" that Jefferson was not a theist.

31. *Ibid.*, p. 1400. Apparently Roger Williams' works were practically unknown during the last quarter of the eighteenth century, so his ideas played little part during this seedtime of the Republic. See LeRoy Moore, Jr., "Roger Williams and the Historians," in *Church History*, XXXII (1963), 33; and "Religious Liberty: Roger Williams and the Revolutionary Era," in *Church History*, XXXIV (1965), 62.

32. McLoughlin, *Isaac Backus and the American Pietistic Tradition*, p. xi.

33. McLoughlin, "Isaac Backus and the Separation of Church and State in America," p. 1402.

34. In his *Common-place Book*, presumably *c*. 1765, Jefferson had explored the question historically and at length, coming to the conclusion that "we may safely affirm (though contradicted by all the judges and writers on earth) that Christianity neither is, nor ever was a part of the common law," in Padover, *The Complete Jefferson*, p. 934.

Fifty-nine years later (June 5, 1824) Jefferson complimented Major John Cartwright, saying, "I was glad to find in your book a formal contradiction, at length, of the judiciary usurpation of legislative powers; for such the judges have usurped in their repeated decisions, that Christianity is a part of the common law." Drawing upon his own earlier researches, Jefferson thought Cartwright's "proof of the contrary . . . incontrovertible; to wit, that the common law existed while the Anglo-Saxons were yet Pagans, at a time when they had never yet heard the name of Christ pronounced, or knew that such a character had ever existed." Showing great historical ingenuity, he then traces the development through English history, concluding that "thus we find this chain of authorities [who have asserted that Christianity is part of the common law] hanging link by link one upon another, and all ultimately on one and the same book, and that a mistranslation of the words 'ancien scripture,' used by Prisot." *Ibid.*, pp. 296-97.

For the vicissitudes and use of the common-law doctrine during the first half of the nineteenth century, see Perry Miller, *The Life of the Mind in America from the Revolution to the Civil War* (New York: Harcourt, Brace & World, Inc., 1965). Book Two; "The Legal Mentality"; Chapter IV, "Law and Morality," pp. 186-206.

35. "Isaac Backus and the Separation of Church and State in America," p. 1400.

36. *Isaac Backus on Church, State, and Calvinism. Pamphlets, 1754-1789* (Cambridge: Belknap Press, 1968), pp. 429, 436.

There is a great deal of at least implied documentation for McLoughlin's position in Martin E. Marty's *Righteous Empire: The Protestant Experience in America* (New York: The Dial Press, 1970). Marty used the word *Evangelical* to describe the "Protestant mainstream" down to c. 1877 in about the same sense as does McLoughlin.

37. *Ibid.*, p. 37.

38. Robert Baird, *Religion in America; . . .* (New York: Harper & Bros., 1845). This is the edition I have used. Because of the numerous citations which follow below, I have for convenience inserted the page references in parentheses in the text.

39. Henry Warner Bowden, ed., *Religion in America: a Critical Abridgement with Introduction* (New York: Harper & Row, 1970), p. xiii.

40. Mr. Bowden, editor of the admirable abridgement of Baird's *Religion in America,* noted that "Baird's treatment of the ideas and circumstances leading to a separation of religious organizations and civil authority did not contain any theological arguments to favor that end," indeed he "was not interested in marshalling theological tenets to defend" separation. *Religion in America: a Critical Abridgement . . . ,* pp. xxvi-xxvii.

41. He was also happy to note that in every state "the publication of licentious books and pictures, profane swearing, blasphemy, obscenity, the interruption of public worship" etc., "are punishable by the laws." And from whence did men learn thus to level their laws against such things? ". . . from the Bible, and nowhere else" (125).

42. Horace Bushnell, *Christian Nurture* (New York: Scribner's, 1903), p. 10.

43. "Reverses Needed," July 1861. In *The Spirit in Man: Sermons and Selections* (New York: Scribner's, 1910), pp. 159-84. And "Popular Government by Divine Right," November, 1864, in

Building Eras in Religion (New York: Scribner's, 1910), pp. 286-318.

For an extended explication of Bushnell's views in this connection, see Howard A. Barnes, "The Idea That Caused a War: Horace Bushnell Versus Thomas Jefferson," *The Journal of Church and State*, XVI, 1 (1974), 73-83.

For extensive treatment of the general context of Bushnell's attitudes, see George M. Fredrickson, *The Inner Civil War: Northern Intellectuals and the Crisis of the Union* (New York: Harper & Row, 1966); Bushnell is specifically treated pp. 25-26, 75-76, 137-41.

44. The quotations are from "Popular Government by Divine Right," pp. 289-90. Hereafter the pages will be put in parentheses in the text, "PG" designating "Popular Government by Divine Right," and "RN" designating "Reverses Needed."

45. This is spelled out by Howard A. Barnes, in "The Idea That Caused a War . . . ," p. 81.

46. For delineation of the concepts of "The ascending [i.e., from the bottom up] and descending [i.e., from the top down] themes of government," see Walter Ullmann, *Principles of Government and Politics in the Middle Ages* (New York: Barnes & Noble, 1966), pp. 19-26.

CHAPTER V

1. Henry F. May, "The Recovery of American Religious History," in *The American Historical Review*, LXX, 1 (October, 1964), 79-92.

2. H. L. Mencken, an editorial in *The American Mercury*, IV (1925), 286.

3. Alfred North Whitehead dated the beginnings of the decline of theology with "the great Methodist movement" (meaning more of course than the Methodist church) which "was singularly devoid of new ideas, and singularly rich in vivid feelings. It is the first decisive landmark indicating the widening chasm between the theological tradition and the modern intellectual world." Unlike previous movements in Christendom, "from the earliest Greek theologians" to the Wesleys' day, Methodism "can appeal to no

great intellectual construction explanatory of its modes of under-standing." Perhaps, Whitehead concluded, it has "chosen the better way." But however we may evaluate the change, "It was a notable event in the history of ideas when the clergy of the western races began to waver in their appeal to constructive reason." More recently, he wryly remarked, "scientists and critical philosophers have followed the Methodist example." *Adventures of Ideas* (New York: Free Press, 1967), pp. 22-23.

In 1959 Jacques Barzun spelled out the results to date of what Whitehead had noted in 1933, in *The House of Intellect* (New York: Harper & Bros., 1959). His argument is briefly, albeit not adequately summed up on a dust-jacket blurb: "How intellect, the prime force in Western civilization, is being destroyed by our culture in the name of art, science and philanthropy."

4. It has been suggested, and we should not rule out the possi-bility, that this kind of madness is inherent in the civilization of Christendom. Samuel Butler observed that "all countries have, and have had, a law of the land, and also another law, which, though professedly more sacred, has far less effect on their daily life and actions. It seems as though the need for some law over and above, and sometimes even conflicting with, the law of the land, must spring from something that lies deep down in man's nature; indeed, it is hard to think that man could ever have become man at all, but for the gradual evolution of a perception that though this world looms so large when we are in it, it may seem a little thing when we have got away from it." *Erewhon or Over the Range* (New York: Signet Classics, 1960), p. 122. And perhaps John Adams' final conclusion was summed up in his letter to Jefferson on July 16, 1814: ". . . for any thing I know this globe may be, the bedlam . . . of the Universe." In Lester Cappon, ed., *The Adams-Jefferson Letters,* II (New York: Simon & Schuster, 1971), 437. In such a universe the normal and happy person would be the one born with the gift of laughter, and a sense that the world was mad"; Raphael Sabatina, *Scaramouche: A Romance of the French Revolution* (Boston: Houghton Mifflin Co., 1921), p. 3.

5. "Objectives and Methods in Intellectual History," in *Missis-sippi Valley Historical Review,* XLIV (June, 1957), 59-60.

Compare Louis Wirth, ". . . the most important thing, therefore, that we can know about a man is what he takes for granted, and the most elemental and important facts about society are those that are seldom debated and generally regarded as settled." In Wirth's preface to Karl Mannheim, *Ideology and Utopia,* trans. by Louis Wirth and Edward Shils (New York: Harvest Books, 1959), pp. xxii-xxiii.

Also A. N. Whitehead: "All systematic thought must start from presuppositions." It is for this reason that "philosophic truth is to be sought in the presuppositions of language rather than in its express statements. For this reason philosophy is akin to poetry, and both of them seek to express that ultimate good sense which we term civilization." *Modes of Thought* (New York: Capricorn Books, 1958), pp. 2, vii.

Similarly H. Richard Niebuhr developed the concept of "general patterns" of thought that characterize an era, and noted that "to a large extent men may be unconscious of the presence in their minds of such general patterns. Only analysis that penetrates below the surface expressions reveals their presence." "The Idea of Covenant and American Democracy," *Church History,* XXIII (June, 1954), 128.

6. A. N. Whitehead, *Adventures of Ideas,* pp. 12, 5.

7. A. N. Whitehead, *Science and the Modern World* (New York: Free Press, 1967), p. 48.

8. *Ibid.,* p. 4.

9. Herbert J. Muller, *Religion and Freedom in the Modern World* (Chicago: The University of Chicago Press, 1963), p. 7. The quotation should be seen in the context of the entire Chapter I, "Religion and Revolution."

10. Jefferson to Miles King, September 26, 1814, in Norman Cousins, ed., *'In God We Trust': the Religious Beliefs and Ideas of the American Founding Fathers* (New York: Harper & Bros., 1958), p. 144. For the larger context of this letter see Daniel J. Boorstin, *The Lost World of Thomas Jefferson* (New York: Henry Holt and Co., 1948), p. 153.

11. "A Bill for Establishing Religious Freedom" as Jefferson originally introduced it into the Virginia Assembly on June 13, 1779. When it was finally adopted in 1786 some changes were made in the wording. Saul K. Padover, ed., *The Complete Jefferson: . . .* (New York: Duell, Sloan & Pearce, 1943), p. 946.

12. "Resources of the Adversary and Means of Their Destruction," in *Sermons Delivered on Various Occasions* (Boston: T. R. Marvin, 1828), p. 268. The sermon was dated October 12, 1827.

13. Charles Beecher, ed., *Autobiography, Correspondence, Etc. of Lyman Beecher, D.D.*, I (New York: Harper & Bros., 1864), 344.

A detailed account of Beecher's context and experience during this period is in my *Nathaniel William Taylor: A Connecticut Liberal* (Chicago: University of Chicago Press, 1942).

14. Still the best access to Lyman Beecher's life, character and work is the two-volume *Autobiography* put together by his children, edited by his son Charles, and published in 1864. Actually it is not an autobiography in the usual sense, but is made up of Lyman's letters, extracts from many of his sermons and addresses, and not only many of his reminiscences but those of the children. Its format and extent make it at the same time a "warts and all" portrait of a very human being and the self-revelation of a notable family. It should be supplemented by Dr. Vincent Harding's Ph.D. dissertation accepted at the University of Chicago in September 1964: "Lyman Beecher and the Transformation of American Protestantism, 1775-1863." This exhaustive study of 696 pages adds greatly to the information in the *Autobiography* and systematically corrects many of its factual errors.

15. *Autobiography*, II, p. 348.

For me the most plausible and helpful discussion of the nature of "the free will of the creature" is that of Dorothy L. Sayers in *The Mind of the Maker* (New York: Meridian Books, 1956), Chapter V, "Free Will and Miracle." Speaking out of her experience as a writer, the creator of characters, she epitomizes her view in one sentence, saying that all the author's created beings "possess this measure of freedom, namely, that unless the author permits them to develop in conformity with their proper nature, they will cease to be true and living creatures" (p. 72). This seems to me to point exactly to the way Beecher and Jefferson, as representative men of their day, conceived the relation between the Creator and the creature, man.

16. Cambridge Platform, Chapter II, section 2. As in Williston Walker, ed., *The Creeds and Platforms of Congregationalism* (Boston: Pilgrim Press, 1960), p. 204. This now classic volume was first published in 1893.

17. Lyman Beecher, *Sermons Delivered on Various Occasions* (Boston: T. R. Marvin, 1828), p. 142. This collection of sermons preached between 1806 and 1827 and published as a unit in 1828, constitute, I think, the clearest presentation of Beecher's theological system, or "model" as I prefer to call it. Therefore in the following analysis of his perspective I have depended almost exclusively on it. Because this involves innumerable quotations, I have thought best to include page references in parentheses in the text, for example, (SVO 142).

18. This of course is very close to Jefferson's ". . . I suppose belief to be the assent of a mind to an intelligible proposition." Cappon, ed., *The Adams-Jefferson Letters,* II, 368.

Perhaps with Thomas Paine's attack on mystery in *The Age of Reason* in mind, Beecher noted that "the belief of a mystery has been pronounced impossible. No man, it is alleged, can be truly said to believe a proposition, the terms of which he cannot comprehend." In reply Beecher conceded as much, but argued that "the mysteries of revelation are not found among its precepts." "A mystery," he said, "is a *fact,* whose general nature is, in some respects, declared intelligibly; but whose particular manner of existence is not declared, and cannot be comprehended." For example, "God is omnipresent. This proposition announces a mystery. The general intelligible fact declared is, that there is no place where God is not; the mystery respects the particular manner in which the divine Spirit pervades immensity" (OS 154).

19. Beecher might have quoted Sir Thomas Browne (1605-1682): "Thus there are two Books from which I collect my Divinity; besides that written one of GOD, another of His servant Nature, that universal and publick Manuscript, that lies expans'd unto the Eyes of all: those that never saw him in the one, have discover'd Him in the other. This was the Scripture and Theology of the Heathens: the natural motion of the Sun made *them* more admire Him than its supernatural station did the Children of Israel; the ordinary effects of Nature wrought more admiration in *them* than in the other all His Miracles. Surely the Heathens knew better how to joyn and read these mystical Letters than we Christians, . . ." *Religio Medici,* in *The Consolation of Philosophy . . .* (New York: The Modern Library, 1943), p. 337.

20. Edmund Morgan, *The Puritan Dilemma*, 1st ed. (Boston: Little, Brown & Co., 1958).

21. Lyman Beecher, "The Native Character of Man," in *The National Preacher*, II (June, 1827), 7.

22. *Autobiography*, I, p. 339.

23. "The Native Character of Man," p. 3.

24. Reinhold Niebuhr, *The Children of Light and the Children of Darkness* (New York: Scribner's Sons, 1944), p. xi.

25. Abraham Lincoln, Reply to an address by Mrs. Eliza P. Gurney, September [28?] 1862, as in Philip Van Doren Stern, ed., *The Life and Writings of Abraham Lincoln* (New York: Modern Library, 1940), p. 728.

For my interpretation of Lincoln's perspective see my *The Lively Experiment* (New York: Harper & Row, 1963), Chapter V, "Abraham Lincoln's 'Last, Best Hope of Earth': The American Dream of Destiny and Democracy."

26. One of the clearest statements of the ramifications of the meaning of providence in the New England Puritan tradition is found in Urian Oakes' sermon of September 10, 1677, "The Soveraign Efficacy of Divine Providence," as in Perry Miller and Thomas H. Johnson, eds., *The Puritans*, I (New York: Harper & Row, 1963), pp. 350-67. Oakes states the heart of the matter, as *"The great God hath the absolute and infallible Determination of the Successes and Events of all the Operations & Vndertakings of created Agents & Second Causes, in his own Power.* His Counsel and soveraign Will appoints what they shall be, and his Providence (which is not determined by any Second Cause: but is the Determiner of them all) Executes accordingly. And it must needs be so, . . ." (p. 358). It is clear that in this conceptual context God is imminent in everything that happens and therefore study of experienced events is always a clue to His will.

27. Lyman Beecher, *A Plea for the West* (Cincinnati: Truman & Smith, 1835), pp. 8-9.

28. See, for example, Jefferson's letter to John Adams of October 28, 1813, in Cappon, ed., *The Adams-Jefferson Letters*, pp. 287-92.

29. Philip Schaff, in the milder terms of peaceful development, spoke of America as *"the grave of all European nationalities;* but a

Phenix grave, from which they shall rise to new life and new activity in a new and essentially Anglo-Germanic form''; in *America: a Sketch of Its Political, Social, and Religious Character*, ed. by Perry Miller (Cambridge, Mass.: The Belknap Press of Harvard University Press, 1961), p. 51.

30. *Lectures on Political Atheism* (London: Clarke, Beeton & Co., n.d.).

31. For a brief but lucid exposition of the religious-political atmosphere of this period, with reference to most of the pertinent literature, see Gary B. Nash, ''The American Clergy and the French Revolution,'' in *William and Mary Quarterly*, XXII (July, 1965), 392-412. I dealt extensively with the period in my dissertation, published as *Nathaniel William Taylor 1786-1858: A Connecticut Liberal*.

32. See the note on Albert Camus's *The Rebel . . .* , (Chapter I, note #14) for comment on this development.

33. For recent commentary on this principle see my *The Nation with the Soul of a Church* (New York: Harper & Row, 1975), pp. 95ff.

34. Compare Jefferson to John Adams, January 1816: ''public opinion'' has been erected ''into a Censor'' until ''opinion is power''; Cappon, ed., *The Adams-Jefferson Letters*, pp. 458, 460. Adams agreed, and thought that now ''public opinion . . . must in some degree be respected by all''; *Ibid.*, p. 461. Adams had said that America was ''a Country where Popularity had more Omnipotence than the British Parliament assumed''; *Ibid.*, p. 356.

35. Lyman Beecher, *Lectures on Political Atheism*, p. 100.

36. That Beecher's sense of urgency was rooted in a realistic assessment of the situation is reflected in such passages as the following. ''In a despotic government, force may protect us where public sentiment is too corrupt to secure the execution of the laws. But in a republic it is not so. There, when public sentiment falters, the laws have no powers and then, first anarchy and next despotism ensues. The genius of our government and the competitions of party have introduced universal suffrage. The door is wide open to all who are born and to all who immigrate, and cannot be shut. We must live by universal suffrage or perish. If we can imbue with knowledge and virtue the mass, we shall live; but if irreligion and profligacy predominate, sure as the march of time we fail.'' *Lectures on Political Atheism*, p. 100.

37. Beecher stoutly resisted the efforts to make them so, in *A Plea for Voluntary Societies . . . Against the Strictures of the Princeton Reviewers and Others* (New York: John S. Taylor, 1837).

38. Compare Madison's views of the place of interest groups and coalitions in the "compound" or "extended republic of the United States," in the fifty-first Federalist Paper.

For my exposition of the principle of the plurality of principles see *The Nation with the Soul of a Church,* pp. 109–23.

39. Charles Beecher, ed., *Autobiography . . . ,* Vol. I, p. 241.

40. This view was stated clearly by Urian Oakes in his sermon of 1677: accepting the dogma that *"God* is the Absolute First Cause, *and Supream Lord of all"* it follows *"That all the Ataxy,* Disorder, Irregularity, moral Evil *that is found in the Actions of Rational Agents, is by His Permission. If it were not the pleasure of God to permit it, no Sin should be in the World, nor in the Actions of Men.* Though there is no *Legal* permission, or allowance of it; (for the Law of God forbids it) yet there is a *Providential* Permission of it." "The Soveraign Efficacy of Divine Providence," as in Perry Miller and Thomas H. Johnson, *The Puritans,* I, pp. 358–59.

41. Beecher's exuberant sermonic description of the efficacy of such "local voluntary associations" is worth quoting at length. "They awaken the public attention, and by the sermons, the reports, and the conversation they occasion, diffuse much moral instruction; they combine the wisdom and influence of all who desire to prevent crimes, and uphold peace and good order in society; they have great influence to form correctly the public opinion, and to render the violation of the law disgraceful, as well as dangerous; they teach the virtuous part of the community their strength, and accustom them to act, as well as to wish and to pray; they constitute a sort of disciplined moral militia, prepared to act upon every emergency, and repel every encroachment upon the liberties and morals of the State. By their numbers, they embolden the timid, and intimidate the enemy; and in every conflict, the responsibility being divided among many, is not feared. By this auxiliary band the hands of the magistrate are strengthened, the laws are rescued from contempt, the land is purified, the anger of the Lord is turned away, and his blessing and protection restored."

42. Cushing Strout, *The New Heavens and New Earth* (New York: Harper and Row, 1974), p. x.

Index

DATE DUE

8 13 '81	
DEC 15 '90	
JUN 1 5 '92	
AUG 3 0 1997	
AUG 0 5 1997	